DAVID MAMET

The Spanish Prisoner AND The Winslow Boy

David Mamet was born in Chicago in 1947. He studied at Goddard College in Vermont and at the Neighborhood Playhouse School of Theater in New York. He has taught at Goddard College, the Yale Drama School, and New York University, and lectures at the Atlantic Theater Company, of which he is a founding member. He is the author of the acclaimed plays *The Cryptogram, Oleanna, Speed-the-Plow, Glengarry Glen Ross, American Buffalo,* and *Sexual Perversity in Chicago.* He has also written screenplays for films such as *Homicide, House of Games, Wag the Dog,* and the Oscar-nominated *The Verdict.* His plays have won the Pulitzer Prize and the Obie Award.

The SPANISH PRISONER

AND

The WINSLOW BOY

The SPANISH PRISONER

AND

The WINSLOW BOY

TWO SCREENPLAYS

DAVID MAMET

VINTAGE BOOKS

A DIVISION OF RANDOM HOUSE, INC.

NEW YORK

CONTENTS

PREFACE

Here are two screenplays. *The Spanish Prisoner* is a rather straightforward Light Thriller, and if such a designation did not previously exist, perhaps it does now.

I cite *The Lady Vanishes* and *Young and Innocent,* both early Hitchcock, and films in which he was working out the balance between comedy and thriller (these earlier films coming down a little heavier on the side of comedy). The paradigm of the genre, of course, is *North by Northwest;* and, perhaps, Stanley Donen's *Charade.* In these the hero (in *Charade,* the heroine) is enmeshed in a situation not of his own making and beyond his understanding. He must, through trial and disappointment, discover that supposed foes are friends and vice-versa, and will, at the end, emerge shaken and stirred to re-examine the benefits of a previous state of innocence. Good fun.

I can take no credit for *The Winslow Boy* whatever. It is a work of melodramatic genius by Terence Rattigan.

Film is *essentially* a melodramatic medium—it appeals to and involves the emotions with depictions of the emotional. Great melodrama, as Stanislavsky told us, is just tragedy *slightly* manqué. It flutters at the intersection of the *exploration of circumstance* and the *exploration of the human condition.*

The Winslow Boy is a great play, and it is, I think, a derogation to speak of Rattigan's "craftsmanship," as it would be to say of Picasso, "Wonderful use of blue."

I love the play, and was thrilled to work on it.

I hope you enjoy these screenplays.

The

SPANISH

PRISONER

A SCREENPLAY

FADE IN:

1. INT. JAMAICA AIRPORT. DAY.

ANGLE, INS.
A large sign reads: "Did you pack your own bag? Are you carrying gifts or packages for anyone you do not know? Has your bag been out of your sight since you packed it?"
   We see a security X-ray screen and several items going through it. Beyond it we see the arrivals area, the ramp pushed up to a jetliner.

2. EXT. ARRIVALS AREA, JAMAICA AIRPORT. DAY.
A young man, around thirty, JOE ROSS, *in too-heavy city clothes, getting down from the first-class ramp on a jetliner, loosens his tie, squints against the sun. He is followed by* GEORGE LANG, *a man of similar age. He proceeds into the airport.*

3. INT. AIRPORT. DAY.
The PASSENGERS *exiting the immigration area. A group of* JAPANESE TOURISTS *before them.* JOE ROSS *comes up to a concession stand.*
ROSS: I'd like a Cuban cigar please . . .
A YOUNG WOMAN, *behind the stand, straightens up and looks at him. She is stunningly beautiful and has a small mole on the side of her mouth. She smiles knowingly at him.*
   ANOTHER WOMAN *comes up to the stand and points at her watch, and the* BEAUTIFUL WOMAN *smiles over her*

shoulder at ROSS, *shrugs to say, "Well, what might have been . . . ," and starts to leave the stand.* GEORGE LANG *walks up behind* ROSS.

LANG: . . . and, um . . . *(He searches for something to keep her there.)* . . . and a *camera* . . .

LANG *picks up a disposable camera. The* BEAUTIFUL WOMAN *disappears through a door in the back of the concession stand. The* OTHER SALESGIRL *hands him a camera.*

SALESGIRL: . . . anything else, sir . . . ?

ROSS: *(Sighs)* The cigar, please, a Cuban cigar.

LANG: Ain't that illegal . . . ?

ROSS: Not down here . . .

LANG: Well, that's the attitude I like. Step out, enjoy yourself.

ROSS: Good advice.

LANG: *I'll* bill you . . . gimme half of that cigar.

ROSS: I'll give you half of the whole adventure.

LANG: And I'll do the same for you.

A stream of JAPANESE TOURISTS *passes behind him.*

WOMAN'S VOICE: *(OS)* . . . Mr. Ross . . .

ROSS *turns and is greeted with a photo flash going off in his face. His vision clears.*

ANGLE.

He has just had his photo taken by a very pretty American woman in her twenties, who is carrying baggage, obviously just off the plane (SUSAN RICCI).

ROSS: . . . *Susan.* You on the plane . . . ?

SALESGIRL: . . . what brand, sir . . . ?

SUSAN: *(Of her camera)* . . . wanted to capture your First Moment on Vacation.

ROSS: *(To the* SALESGIRL*)* . . . anything good.

She hands him a cigar.

SALESGIRL: . . . that is eight dollars US.

SUSAN: Yes. I was on the plane. Back in the Cheap Seats.
    While the Stars sat up front. Isn't it beautiful down
    here, Mr. Ross . . . ?

LANG: Well, I don't know, Susan. We've only seen the *air-
    port.*

ROSS *picks up the cigar, and* LANG *picks up the camera.*

SUSAN: *(Pointing at the camera)* . . . didn't know you were
    the Tourist Type.

ROSS: He isn't. He's just "trolling" . . .

They start out of the airport.

LANG: 'D you pay eight bucks for that cigar . . . ?

ROSS: . . . taste for the High Life.

LANG: Well, God knows you deserve it.

ROSS: . . . that's right.

LANG: *God* knows, and now you've got to be sure
    everyone *else* knows . . .

ROSS: *(Smiles)* Wish I knew how.

Camera has taken them to a baggage claim area. SUSAN
starts picking up bags off the conveyor.

LANG: Let me help you with your bags . . .

SUSAN: Oh, no, Mr. Lang. That wouldn't be right . . .

ROSS: *(Of bags on the conveyor)* Oh. And here they are:
    The Dog and Pony Show . . .

ANGLE.

Two large yellow cases coming off the conveyor. SUSAN
moves to them.

SUSAN: Oh, no. I told Mr. Klein I'd take these myself . . .

LANG: *(To* ROSS, *sotto)* 'Nything sensitive innem?

ROSS *shakes his head.*

   LANG *nods, meaning "good work."*

4. INT. CONFERENCE ROOM, BARCLAY HOUSE. DAY.
*A spanking new motor yacht, two hundred feet long, a
helicopter on its fantail. It is in a pristine Caribbean
lagoon. A white-coated* JAMAICAN WAITER *comes into the
shot, pushing a room service tray. Camera moves with
him to reveal the two large yellow boxes on a conference
table, and several* SIXTYISH TYPES. LANG *is standing next
to a display board, over which a sheet has been draped.
All await the exit of the* WAITER. *The* WAITER *leaves.*
LANG *is about to speak.* ROSS *gestures "one moment,"
goes to the window, and closes the shutters.* LANG *un-
covers the board and continues in his speech to the*
BUSINESSMEN.

LANG: . . . the Process. And, by the *means* of the Process,
to control of the Global Market.

BUSINESSMAN: . . . and the team, which . . .

LANG: . . . the *team,* Mr. *Ross's* team, and I think, Mr.
Klein, if I may, it would not be amiss to state that the
bulk of the work, and the bulk of the *inspiration* for
the Process . . .

KLEIN: *(A businessman type, rising)* Thank you, George, I
think that you'll understand if I say that that's neither
Here nor There; these gentlemen have come here to
Hear the Good News . . . and the Good News is that
this Process is going to . . . *(He gestures to* ROSS.*)* And
these are *your* figures . . . going to generate for the
Company, a windfall on the order of . . .

*He strides to the blackboard and writes a figure, unseen to
the camera but seen by the* BUSINESSMEN, *several of whom
gasp.*

BUSINESSMAN: . . . and how long can we hold on to it,
before the Japanese . . .

KLEIN: . . . well, we defined it, tooth and nail, it's a proprietary process, we . . .

BUSINESSMAN: *(Nods)* . . . of course, after-the-fact, but the
    Japanese . . .
KLEIN: Well, we have, we have tight security, but, to speak
    to your point . . . Joe . . . ?
LANG: . . . the legal issues are these: we have a de facto and
    de jure copyright in the Process, it was developed for
    us by . . .
He nods at ROSS, *who nods back.*

5. EXT. CONFERENCE ROOM. DAY.
The group of BUSINESSMEN *emerging from the room. The
window is thrown open to reveal the yacht in the lagoon.
We see we are in an extraordinarily posh hotel, a series of
bungalows connected by breezeways and verandas.
White-coated* WAITERS *carrying fruit drinks. Camera
moves into the conference room, past the emerging* BUSI-
NESSMEN, *where* ONE *of their group has stayed behind to
interrogate* LANG *and* ROSS. *He puts his arm around* ROSS.
BUSINESSMAN: Want to thank you, Young Fella.
ROSS: Pleasure, sir . . .
BUSINESSMAN: And I believe you'll see our thanks
    expressed at the Next Stockholders' Meeting, in New
    York . . . *(He gestures to the yellow cases, which*
    LANG *is packing up.)* You keeping this thing under
    wraps, I trust.
ROSS: *(Of the cases)* No sensitive material here, sir.
KLEIN *reenters the room.*
KLEIN: No sensitive material anywhere outside of the New
    York Office. *(He shows a key on a chain around his
    neck.)* Two keys. Mr. Ross and me.

6.
*The group of four start out of the conference room. Cam-
era tracks with them.*

KLEIN: And we find that the best way to keep a secret is
     Don't Tell Nobody . . .
BUSINESSMAN: Waal, let's keep it that way . . .
*Camera tracks through a lovely, open lobby area, with a
sign on the wall reading, "Barclay House, Jamaica, Estab-
lished 1824." SUSAN is sitting in the lobby area. KLEIN ges-
tures, and LANG hands her the yellow display boxes. KLEIN
turns to LANG and ROSS.*
KLEIN: Thank you, Gents. Beautifully done . . .
He starts away. ROSS buttonholes him.
KLEIN: Hope you enj——
ROSS: Mr. Klein, 'f I might: They were kind enough to
     mention the Stockholders' Meeting, but: If I could
     discuss the exact *terms* of my . . .
KLEIN: . . . of your . . . ?
ROSS: . . . of, of my *bonus* . . .
KLEIN: *(Laughing)* I'm in the same position as you, lad—
     they keep *me* in the dark, *too.* Y'need a couple of
     bucks for the rent . . . ?
*He mimes putting his hand in his pocket. Camera tracks
with them as they walk. They stop by a tennis court.*
ROSS: "For the Rent." I can't say that I do, sir. No, but . . .
KLEIN: Joe, tell you what . . . I'm down here to enjoy
     myself. Frankly, that's why we brought you fellas
     down here, too, give you a "perk." You want to dis-
     cuss business, New York. My Office. Any time . . .
*Two very lovely YOUNG WOMEN are walking off the tennis
court.*
KLEIN: *(Of the young women)* Looks like there's lots to do
     down here . . . *(He winks.)* See y'in New York.
*The two YOUNG WOMEN walk past. As they are parting,
one says to the other.*
YOUNG WOMAN: *(With a British accent)* Bar, seven o'clock.

As she does so, she looks back over her shoulder at ROSS.
SECOND YOUNG WOMAN: In the Bar s'en o'clock, see you
     there . . .

ANGLE.
ROSS, *who is standing in front of a very posh "resort"
clothing store, looking at the* WOMEN. LANG *walks up to
him.* ROSS, *in a daze, turns to look at* LANG.
ROSS: . . . said if I needed some help with the Rent, he
     could help me out.
LANG: Well, that's why they're called "the rich." Joe . . .
Pause.
ROSS: "He's in the Same Position as Me."
LANG, *indicating the* YOUNG WOMEN, *who are retreating in
the distance.*
LANG: Well, not quite, cause he's got thirty years on you.
     (Pause) Tell you what: let's dress up and chase after
     beautiful Young Women . . . *That'll* teach 'em . . .
     they say The Bar, at Seven o'clock . . . ?
ROSS: *(Looking down at himself)* I didn't bring any
     clothes.
LANG: Well, you see, that was your mistake. And what you
     have to do is *reinvent* yourself. Because the *Girls*
     come to Money, and the *money* comes to Money, and
     you got to, at least, *look* like money . . .
*He points to the clothing store behind him and begins to
exit.*
LANG: The Baaa, at Seven . . .
He snaps a photo of ROSS *with the disposable camera and
throws it to* ROSS, *who catches it and puts it in his pocket.*

7. INT. HOTEL LOBBY. DAY.
ROSS *comes up to the counter, extracting his wallet.*

ROSS: I'd like to exchange some traveler's checks,
    please . . . ?
He is gestured back into the office, behind the counter.

8. ANGLE. INT. THE OFFICE. DAY.
*The office is small, Colonial-Caribbean-British. On the
wall, several wall-mounted TV security cameras.* ROSS
*starts signing checks, and he looks up at a camera show-
ing the yacht and the steps down to the dock.* SUSAN *is
escorted into the office by another hotel* FUNCTIONARY.
SUSAN: *(To the* FUNCTIONARY*)* . . . both the room charges,
    and the incidentals of . . .
FUNCTIONARY: . . . we were told the incidental expenses
    were to be billed to the individual guests.
SUSAN: . . . fit of generosity, boss changed his mind.
FUNCTIONARY: . . . I will need you to sign . . .
SUSAN: Except, of course, the *telephone* calls, which . . .
The FUNCTIONARY *starts into a back office.* SUSAN *lingers
for a moment and glances up at the TV screen showing the
yacht.*
SUSAN: . . . some paddleboat, eh?
SUSAN *exits.*
CLERK: *(To the* FUNCTIONARY*)* Annie, you have to change
    the tapes on the video . . .
ROSS: What do you keep the tapes for?
CLERK: Insurance company demands it. People Water-
    skiing, and so on. In case of a suit.
The DESK CLERK *starts counting out the money.*
CLERK: A lot of money, sir, they'd give you a better
    exchange at the bank.
ROSS: No, I need it now. I'm reinventing myself.

9. EXT. CLOTHING STORE. DUSK.
A TAILOR *holding several garments in his arms nods to*

ROSS, *who is togged out head to foot in new, very fashion-able tropical clothes.* ROSS *comes out of the store. He runs into* SUSAN, *camera around her neck.*

SUSAN: Oh, Lord, don't you look fine.

ROSS: Clothes make the man.

SUSAN: Got to take a picture, to show them back at the office . . . *(She snaps a photo of him.)* . . . how'd the meeting go . . . ?

He holds up a finger, to caution "silence."

SUSAN: . . . something big, huh, that's what they all think back at the Office. Something Big.

ROSS: . . . something Big.

SUSAN: Um. Planning a Big Night tonight? To Celebrate . . . ?

ROSS: *(Smiles)* Might be.

A JAPANESE COUPLE *walks in front of them.*

SUSAN: Uh huh. Did you know Jamaica is the number-one Honeymoon Destination for young Japanese?

ROSS: *(Smiles)* I didn't know that.

SUSAN: Well. It is. Long way to come. *(Pause.)* Must be because it's so Romantic.

He tries to extricate himself from her gently and moves toward the beach, where he begins taking photos with his little disposable camera.

SUSAN: . . . and I *thought*, if, um . . . Mr. Ross . . . "Joe," if you didn't, um . . .

Beyond them, in the lagoon, a small launch is coming from the yacht. In it are a middle-aged MAN *and a very beautiful* YOUNG GIRL. *A* BODYGUARD TYPE *stays with the launch.*

ROSS: *(Checks his watch)* Uh, well, actually, I have some *things* to do tonight . . .

SUSAN: Oh, no, I understand . . . I understand. But if, you know, you get your work *done* early, or . . .

ROSS: *(Smiling)* Thank you very much.

She, awkward, steps back and takes his photograph.

SUSAN: . . . lovely new clothes.

ROSS: It's good of you to say so.

SUSAN: Well . . .

She makes an exit. ROSS *turns back toward the lagoon, where the* MAN *and the* GIRL *from the yacht's launch are coming up the stairs. Two lovely* YOUNG WOMEN *are coming up from the beach. They pass in front of the* MAN *and the* GIRL *from the yacht.* ROSS *gestures to the* YOUNG WOMEN.

ROSS: *(Snaps a photo)* Hold it . . . Thank you. Hello.

FIRST GIRL: . . . hello.

ROSS: Yes. Where are you girls from . . . ?

SECOND GIRL: . . . where are we "from"?

ROSS: Um, yes . . .

SECOND GIRL: Well . . .

The MAN *from the yacht leaves his* COMPANION, *who is wearing a large picture hat, in the BG and comes over to* ROSS.

MAN FROM YACHT: I'll give you a thousand dollars for that camera.

Pause.

ROSS: . . . *what?*

MAN FROM YACHT: I'll give you five thousand dollars if you give me that camera . . .

ROSS: *(Playing to the* TWO GIRLS*)* Well, you know, if it's *important* to you, take it . . . I don't need your money . . . *take* it . . .

He hands the camera to the MAN *from the yacht. The other* TWO GIRLS, *unsure of what is going on, retreat* . . .

ROSS: Take it. My compliments.

The MAN *takes the camera. He and the* YOUNG WOMAN *in the picture hat move off.* ROSS *looks at the* YOUNG WOMAN *as she and the* MAN *from the yacht move off.*

10. EXT. HOTEL VERANDA. DUSK.

ROSS, *in new sport coat and trousers, looking very posh, walks. Camera follows him into an open-air bar area. Various wealthy-looking couples and* ROSS, *who seats himself at the bar and looks at his watch. He looks around the bar, anticipatorily.*

SUSAN: *(VO)* . . . a very hush-hush "secret" development, but *I'm* so low down the Food Chain . . .

ROSS *turns to see* SUSAN, *in an angle of the bar, talking with a* WOMAN *in her late twenties.* SUSAN *turns to* ROSS.

SUSAN: Oh. Hello, Joe. I was just . . .

ROSS: *(Instructing her)* Yeah, we're Secret Agents down here, superrich and powerful, re-forming the world. And full of priceless Information.

WOMAN AT THE BAR: . . . everybody on vacation's got a story, innit . . . ?

ROSS: That's right. Everybody likes to Feel Important. *(He looks meaningfully at* SUSAN. *To the* WOMAN *at the bar)* And what do *you* do . . . ?

WOMAN AT THE BAR: Me . . . ? I'm with the FBI.

They all laugh. The WOMAN *at the bar excuses herself and moves off.*

   Pause.

SUSAN: I shoul'na said anything. . . . not that I *know* anything . . . you're right. *You're* right. . . . you know what I have? A Secretary Mentality. That's what I have.

ROSS *is scanning the bar. He sees* LANG *enter and gets up from his stool at the bar.*

ROSS: No, that's right, Susan, it might be a good idea if you were to . . .

SUSAN: Not that anyone *tells* me anything, I'm here to Fetch and Carry.

ROSS: Would you excuse me?

He walks over to LANG.

LANG: *(Of* SUSAN*)* Somebody's gotta crush on you.

ROSS: Would you explain what's *wrong* with me?

LANG: Ain't nothing wrong with you. I'm going to tell you
    something: your *ship* comes in, and it *has* come in,
    you're going to be whisking 'em away like *flies.* Just
    like Flies. Nice shirt.

ROSS: . . . my ship comes in.

LANG: Your ship has come in. They can twist and squirm,
    but the Company owes you So Big . . .

ROSS: . . . and if they don't pay . . . ?

LANG: Well: Alright: Nobody likes to part with money. But
    here's what I think:

His eyes light up. The two YOUNG WOMEN *from the tennis
court show up, in evening dresses.* LANG, *followed by*
ROSS, *detaches himself from the bar and proceeds toward
them.* LANG *introduces himself to a* YOUNG WOMAN *and is
about to present the other to* ROSS *when a* YOUNG MAN *in
U.S. naval officer's dress whites appears and is obviously
the* SECOND WOMAN'*s escort.* ROSS *bows himself out and
moves away. In the BG we see* LANG *gesture "Tough luck."*
ROSS *starts back toward the bar. He is about to sit when
he sees* SUSAN *advancing on the bar, and he starts to slip
away from her. In the BG we see* KLEIN *and his table of*
BUSINESSMEN. KLEIN *waves desultorily toward* ROSS. ROSS
*nods back. He picks up a cigar from a humidor at the end
of the bar and gestures at the* BARMAN, *"Write it down."*

11. EXT. TENNIS COURTS. NIGHT.

ROSS *lighting his cigar. He turns and looks down the hill at
the yacht moored in the lagoon.*

MAN ON YACHT: *(VO)* Y'interested in Tennis . . . ?

ROSS *turns to see the* MAN ON THE YACHT.

ROSS: Play a little. Never had too much time for it.

MAN ON YACHT: Well, that's the whole problem with the whole thing, isn't it? Man said: It's alright when your hobbies get in the way of your work, but when they start to get in the way of each *other* . . . *(He laughs to himself.)* My little *sister* plays tennis. *(Pause)* Alternate on the Olympic Team . . . waaal, alright, what I want to say is "thank you." *(Pause)* I was wrong today.

ROSS *starts to interrupt.*

MAN ON YACHT: I was wrong to offer you *money*, and . . . and I appreciate your gesture, and I am in your debt. Thank you. *(He offers his hand.)*

ROSS: Glad to help.

Two young JAPANESE WOMEN *in kimonos walk by, laughing.* ROSS *looks at them. The* MAN ON THE YACHT *remarks* ROSS *watching.*

MAN ON YACHT: Lovely Romantic Spot.

The WOMEN *walk up to two* MEN, *obviously their husbands.*

MAN ON YACHT: Everybody comes down here in Pairs. If you would like to meet some people . . . um. Tomorrow night, if you'd like to come on the boat . . .

He gestures at his yacht.

ROSS: Oh. That's very kind. I've got to be back in New York tomorrow . . .

MAN ON YACHT: *(Nods)* My name is Julian Dell, by the way.

ROSS: *(Extending his hand)* Joseph Ross.

They shake hands. The two start to stroll off.

DISSOLVE TO:

12. EXT. HOTEL TERRACE. DAWN.

TWO MEN *seated, their coats over the backs of the chairs. An empty bottle and two glasses on a table between them,*

as they look out over the yacht. The helicopter is now
gone.

JIMMY: *(As he gestures at the walkway, where he and the*
     YOUNG WOMAN *were photographed)* . . . a
     "princess" . . . she's a "princess," you might say that
     the title means nothing, as the "country" hardly
     exists anymore. But perhaps it means something . . .

ROSS: I think it means something.

JIMMY: *(Pause)* I do, too.

Pause.

ROSS: . . . and . . . she's *(searching for an answer)* she's
     underage . . . ?

JIMMY: Waal, she's *married.* And she's married to a *friend*
     of mine, and I'm a cad and a rotter, so I saw you with
     the *camera* . . . *(He gestures to the yacht.)* D'you
     want to come back and get some breakfast on the . . .
     no, they'll all still be ashore . . .

A WAITER *passes by.*

JIMMY: Excuse me . . . excuse me . . . could we get a pot of
     coffee, do you think . . . ?

ROSS: . . . what happened to the Princess?

JIMMY: What happened to her? Well, she was, of course,
     never *here,* so we had to whisk her back to her Hus-
     band.

He gestures at the yacht, makes a "helicopter" gesture. As
they look out, a young COUPLE *walks, arms around each*
other, down the beach.

JIMMY: That's the trouble with these spots, eh? Everyone
     comes down in *pairs* . . .

ROSS: That's *true.*

JIMMY: Well, I *know* it's true—but I tell you what: come
     out to the rowboat for dinner tonight, and I'll . . .
     No, y're going back to New York. *Why're* you going
     back to New York . . . ?

ROSS: Got to Pay the Rent.

JIMMY: Ha. *(Pause)* My *sister* says: "They only want me for my money . . ." I tell her, Praise God and Thank your Lucky *Stars*. 'F yo're going to let it *control* you . . . what's the point of it? Which is why, by the way, she always *ends* up with Fortune Hunters . . . oh—Tell you a story. Fellow came to me, a proposition, said, "I need a half hour of your time, and it will *make* you *(He picks a figure out of the air.)* fifty million dollars." *I* said, Fifty million dollars, a half hour. That's one hundred million for an hour, that's four billion a week, that's two hundred billion a year, assuming I would take a two-week vacation. *He* said: 'f you were making that much a week, you couldn't *afford* to take a vacation . . .

As they are laughing, LANG, *after what was obviously a hard night, staggers past. He stops and looks at the two. Beat.*

LANG: . . . good morning.

ROSS: George Lang, Julian Dell.

LANG: . . . fella with the Boat.

JIMMY: That's right.

LANG: A pleasure . . . *(He continues off.)* Nice boat . . .

JIMMY *gets up, stretches, looks around, looks out at his yacht.*

JIMMY: Fella said, We must never forget that we are Human. And, as humans, we must dream. And when we dream . . . we dream of money . . . *(He looks out at his yacht and shakes his head.)* Money: *Impresses* everybody, what did it ever do for one?

ROSS: . . . useful if you want to *buy* things.

JIMMY: *(Nods. Pause)* . . . *some* people . . . *(Pause)* It makes them frightened. *(To himself)* . . . makes 'em frightened to leave the house . . . my *sister* . . .

ROSS: Is she Young and Pretty?

JIMMY: . . . she's the closest thing to my heart in the
World. *(He recollects himself.)* Oh, yes, I think she'd
qualify as Young and Pretty . . . waaaaallll . . . going
to take a walk. Want to take a walk . . . ?

ROSS: Bedtime for me.

JIMMY: Well, then, perhaps, we'll meet back in New York.
Got a card . . . ?

ROSS *hands him a card.* JIMMY *puts it in his pocket.*

JIMMY: Pleasure, Joe.

ROSS: Jimmy . . .

They shake hands.

JIMMY: Lovely gesture of yours, giving me that camera
back . . . *(Pause)* You impress me, sir.

He hesitates, as if he wants to say more, then moves off.
ROSS *props up his feet. The* WAITER *arrives with coffee.*
ROSS *takes out a cigar. The* WAITER *lights it, and* ROSS
*looks out, contentedly, at the lagoon and the yacht, and
puffs on his cigar.*

DISSOLVE TO:

13. EXT. HOTEL. DAY.

A van, a pile of luggage. SUSAN *being walked out of the
reception area by a concierge. She holds the yellow file
boxes.*

SUSAN: . . . bills to the Main Office, and all personal and
incidental items, as we spoke of—*(She gestures,
meaning "Put them on the tab.")*

ROSS: *(VO)* They work you pretty hard.

SUSAN: They work us *all* hard—Good to have a job.

ROSS *comes into the shot.*

SUSAN: *(Looking at her list)* Well, now I *know* they are high on you. They even told me to pick up your Local Calls.

ROSS *passing through the shot.*

ROSS: Wish I'd have been a different kind of guy.

SUSAN: What would you have done?

ROSS: I'd of Gone Hog Wild on the Company, and stolen a Bathrobe.

He turns and walks backwards while talking to her, and he bumps into KLEIN.

KLEIN: . . . the group expressed some anxiety about Insider Trading, and . . .

ROSS: Mr. Klein, I'm not about to indulge in Insider . . .

KLEIN: . . . just mention it as a matter of . . .

ROSS: No, sir, I understan——

LANG *moves past the group, obviously hungover, and gets into the airport van.*

ROSS: Would you excuse me, sir . . . ?

KLEIN: No, I'll see you back in New York.

14. INT. AIRPORT VAN. DAY.

ROSS *sits down next to* LANG.

LANG: Don't talk to me.

ROSS: What'd you do . . . ?

LANG: . . . took me to a Casino . . . stayed up drinking, oh, my Lord . . . *(He clutches his head. He feels in an inside pocket. Extracts a wad of cash.)* What'd *you* do . . . ?

ROSS: Actually I had a rather interesting . . .

LANG *hands a wad of cash to* ROSS.

ROSS: What's this?

LANG: We're partners. You said we were partners—"Split the Adventure Part." Passu—here's your half—

ROSS: I don't want it.

LANG: *(Of the cash)* . . . give it to *Charity.*

He closes his eyes. ROSS *spots something. He gets off the van to help* SUSAN, *who is loading bags into the trunk.*

SUSAN: Thank you. Do you know, you are a real *gentleman.*

ROSS *sees something over her shoulder.*

ROSS: Would you excuse me a moment?

ANGLE, ROSS'S POV.

Running up from the pier, JIMMY, *waving for* ROSS *to stop.* ROSS *moves away from* KLEIN *and down the steps to* JIMMY.

JIMMY: Hey, look here. You're going back to New York, might I ask you a service . . . ?

He hands a small wrapped parcel to ROSS.

ROSS: Certainly.

JIMMY: Could you drop this off for my sister . . . ?
(Points to the address) Mrs. DaSilva. At the San Remo.

ROSS: . . . pleasure.

JIMMY: You don't mind . . . ?

ROSS: Glad to do it.

JIMMY: Do you know, I've got to be in New York Friday. Are you free?

ROSS: . . . I . . .

JIMMY: We'll have dinner. Are you free?

ROSS: Of course.

JIMMY: I'll call you. *(He takes* ROSS's *card out of his pocket, and waves it.)*

ROSS: I'll look forward to it.

JIMMY: *(Waving good-bye)*

The limo van honks.

JIMMY: Friday . . .
ROSS *turns and runs back toward the limo van.*

15. INT. JAMAICA AIRPORT. DAY.
A sign reads, "First-Class Passengers." ROSS *and* LANG *are standing in line.* LANG, *very hungover, eyes closed. They move forward, and* ROSS, *out of the corner of his eye, sees* SUSAN, *weighted down by her packages, struggling through the economy line. As he watches, the "*FBI*"* WOMAN *from the bar comes up to her. They greet each other, the* FBI WOMAN *hands* SUSAN *a business card, and they shake hands.* SUSAN *picks up her packages and struggles forward.*
TICKET AGENT: *(VO)* May I help you, sir . . . ?

ANGLE.
ROSS *comes forward, takes out* LANG's *ticket, takes out his own ticket, and, with it, takes out the wad of cash* LANG *gave him.*
ROSS: . . . do you have any more room in First Class . . . ?

ANGLE.
ROSS *looks back at* SUSAN, *who is struggling in line. He beckons to her, and she starts over to the First-Class line.*

16. INT. AIRPORT. SECURITY AREA. DAY.
SUSAN, LANG, *and* ROSS. SUSAN *goes through the metal detector, and as she does turns back to talk to* ROSS.
SUSAN: . . . this is so generous of you . . .
The metal detector goes off as SUSAN *walks through it.*
SECURITY PERSON: . . . I'm sorry, miss . . . *(She points at* SUSAN.)
SUSAN: . . . the Camera . . . ?
SECURITY PERSON: . . . just put it on the belt . . .

Camera moves onto a sign that reads: "Have you packed your own bags? Have they been out of your sight? Are you carrying a package for someone you don't know . . . ?" In front of the sign are LANG *and* ROSS. LANG *wakes up to the beeping.*

LANG: . . . somebody said, "Nobody going on a business trip would've been missed if he didn't arrive . . ."

SECURITY PERSON: *(In BG. To* SUSAN*)* . . . no, ma'am, it won't hurt the film . . .

ANGLE. FROM BEHIND THE SECURITY COUNTER.

We see the camera, going through the metal detector, on its television screen, and SUSAN, *and the* TWO MEN, *as they pass through the detector.*

17. INT. PLANE. DAY.

The THREE, *coming into the First-Class cabin.* LANG *flops into a seat.*

SUSAN: *(To* ROSS*)* I was just concerned, I didn't want to lose the film . . .

A STEWARDESS *comes up to check* SUSAN's *ticket.*

SUSAN: *(To* ROSS*)* . . . you know, this is so nice of you, really . . . *(She shows her ticket.)* And they told me I even get to keep my return ticket. Use it any time . . . not that I'm likely to get *back* here, but . . .

ANGLE, INS.

The ticket reads, "New York to Jamaica Open." A STEWARDESS *comes up to* SUSAN, *obviously doubting that she belongs in the First-Class cabin.*

STEWARDESS: . . . may I see your ticket, miss . . . ?

SUSAN: No, I know you wouldn't think it, but this gentleman arranged for me to sit here with the quality. *(She*

shows her ticket, and she sits next to ROSS*.)* Shows to
go you. Y'never know who anybody is . . .
ROSS *nods. He takes out some papers from his briefcase
and the package, which we see is addressed: "Mrs. A.
DaSilva. San Remo. New York." He puts the package
back into his briefcase and begins to work on his papers.*
SUSAN: Never know who anybody is. That girl, said she
was with the FBI . . . *guess* what she does . . . ?
STEWARDESS: *(On the intercom)* Ladies and gentlemen, we
will be departing shortly, would you please check to
see that . . . *(Etc.)*
SUSAN: *(Hands a card to* ROSS*)* She *is* with the FBI. Ha.
*He takes the card, reads: "Special Agent Pat McCune.
Federal Bureau of Investigation," etc.*
ROSS: Funny old world.
SUSAN: Funny Old World? Dog my *Cats*?
ROSS: Dog my Cats, indeed.

DISSOLVE TO:

18. INT. PLANE. DAY.
The plane in flight. ROSS *coming back from the front ser-
vice area with a glass of champagne. Passes by* SUSAN,
who is staring at the FBI card.
SUSAN: . . . y'never know who *anybody* is. With the excep-
tion of me. I am what I look like. *(Pause)* Why is that,
Mr. Ross . . . ?
ROSS: I think you look just fine.
SUSAN: No. Anybody could be *Anybody,* mysterious,
or . . . take that guy who got off the yacht. Alright?
Take *him.*
ROSS: What about him . . . ?
SUSAN: What about him, who was he?

ROSS: Uh. *I* don't know . . . he was a fellow got off a
   yacht.
SUSAN: Just my point. Just my point. We *think* he was a
   fellow got off a yacht.
ROSS: You can't go through life mistrusting everybody—
   you mistrust everybody?
SUSAN: No. Just strangers . . .
ROSS: But we saw him get off the yacht.
SUSAN: We did not. We saw him in a boat that came from
   the *direction* of the yacht.
ROSS: I saw him get off the yacht.
SUSAN: Waaall . . . *(She pats her camera.)* I got a picture,
   took a picture of you, and he's in the background,
   and I believe you'll see, I can't say I'm sure, but I
   think you'll see the boat just came around, from the
   direction of the yacht. And we have *no* idea who *anyone* is . . . *(Pause)* 'cept me . . .
STEWARDESS, *coming down the aisle, distributing cards.*
STEWARDESS: We will be landing in New York shortly. You
   are required to fill out a customs form, and immigration form. Non–United States Citizens . . .
LANG *wakes painfully to the* STEWARDESS's *speech. He
takes a card. He beckons* ROSS *over.*
LANG: . . . I think I'm getting the flu. *(Sotto)* I'm taking in
   some Cuban cigars. You? Did you? Where'd you hide
   'em . . . ?
ROSS *moves away from him, back to* SUSAN, *who is filling
out her card and continuing in her speech.*
SUSAN: Like they say at the airport: Did Anyone Give You
   a *Package*, did you, uh . . . did you leave your . . .
ROSS: . . . what do you mean?
SUSAN: Well, what do they call them, uh, Mules? People
   get people to bring in . . . *dope,* uh . . . s'm'b'y give

you a package to take back . . . it, well, you go to a
resort, my *mother* would say *everyone's*
pretending . . .

ANGLE.
On ROSS *as he takes out the package from his briefcase.*

ANGLE, INS.
ROSS's *hands holding the package.*
SUSAN: *Who* is what they seem. Who in this world is what
they seem . . . 'cept me . . .

ANGLE.
ROSS *gets up hurriedly and moves over past* SUSAN, *excus-
ing himself. Hold on the package he holds in his hands as
he moves past the* STEWARDESS . . .
STEWARDESS: Excuse me, sir, we will be landing
moment——
ROSS: . . . yes, I've got to . . .

19. INT. PLANE LAVATORY. DAY.
ROSS *holding the package in his hands. He bolts the door
behind him. The "Return to Cabin" sign is blinking. He
looks at the package. Holds it to his nose and sniffs it. He
hesitates a moment, then tears it open. He looks down.*

ANGLE, INS.
The package holds an old book, and ROSS *has just torn off
the cover. His hands turn the cover, and we read,* Don
Budge—Principles of Tennis. *His hands flip the pages. It is
only an old book. A card falls out of the pages. He holds it
up and reads it. In a man's handwriting, on beautiful card
stock, embossed at the top, "J.D.," it reads: "Ann:*

Thought you'd enjoy this. Also think you will enjoy the bearer, whom I recommend to you as a good fellow. How about seeing someone I approve of for a change? Let's have din. This week, Friday? Love. J."

CAPTAIN: *(VO)* We have started our descent into New York's Kennedy Airport, and we request that all passengers . . .

ANGLE.

ROSS, *holding the torn book, smiles and shakes his head. He begins reassembling the package.*

20. INT. NEW YORK CITY. LIMO. DAY. NEW YORK CITY STREETS.

ANGLE, INS. THE TORN BOOK.

LANG: *(VO)* 'r' are we . . . ?

ANGLE.

LANG, *who is just waking up.* ROSS, *looking down at the book, looks at* LANG.

ROSS: How d'you feel . . . ?

LANG: My imagination, or's it that secretary up with us.

ROSS: You bought her a ticket.

LANG: *I* bought her the ticket . . . *You* bought her the ticket. You know your problem is, Joe? You're Too Nice . . .

ROSS: Mmm.

LANG: Everything for Everybody else. Nothing for Yoursel—— . . . speaking of which: 'N' it's a conflict of interest. But you need to go in there and hold the company up. The Stockholders' Meeting? They're going to cheer about the Process and give you an attaboy.

ROSS: . . . that's . . . that's true.

LANG: Well, if you know it, you should do something about it. 'N' here's what I think you should do:

ROSS *spies something out the window.*

ROSS: Stop the car, please, Driver. *(To LANG)* I'm going to get out here. See you in the off——

LANG: I'm not going to the office. I'm going hhh——. . . . you should do something for *yourself* once in a while.

He extracts a cigar from his lapel pocket and hands it to ROSS.

LANG: Got 'em through customs. Have a cigar.

ANGLE.

Out the car window, we see they have stopped on Lexington Avenue, in front of a shop whose sign reads, "Lexington. Rare Books, Prints, Bookbinding."

ANGLE.

ROSS *getting out of the car, walking into the shop.*

21. INT. LEXINGTON PRINT AND BOOKSHOP. DAY.

A YOUNG WOMAN *standing in the door to a back office. An* OLDER BOOKISH MAN *comes out, carrying* ROSS's *torn book. He is addressing the camera* (ROSS).

BOOKBINDER: *Could,* of course, be rebound . . . but . . .

ROSS: . . . the price is not an issue . . .

BOOKBINDER: Certainly, sir; but, 's I was going to say, it's a common book, common edition . . . *(He beckons the* YOUNG WOMAN *over, shows her the book, and she moves off, nodding.)* I wouldn't be surprised if we . . . by the way; if you're interested in Don Budge . . . *(He walks out from behind his counter and takes* ROSS *to a framed photo and signed letter of Don Budge.)* . . .

happens to be, we have a *very* good autograph of
him, at the French Open in . . .
WOMAN: *(Calling, from a ladder)* . . . got it, Mr. Cole . . .
(She holds up a book.)
BOOKBINDER: Ah, you see, the Very Thing.

ANGLE, INS.
The BOOKBINDER, *holding both the torn and the new
book. The* WOMAN *starts down the ladder.*

22. EXT. THE SAN REMO, CENTRAL PARK WEST. DAY.

ANGLE, INS.
The torn book. ROSS's *hands rearrange it to show, on top,
the package, now rewrapped, marked "Mrs. A. DaSilva,"
etc.*

ANGLE.
The doorway into the San Remo. A very OLD WOMAN
with a walker, accompanied by a young PRACTICAL NURSE,
coming out of the building. The DOORMAN *tips his hat to
her.*

ANGLE.
ROSS, *crossing* CPW *from the park, comes up to the build-
ing and hands the* DOORMAN *the package.*
ROSS: For Mrs. DaSilva.
The DOORMAN *touches his cap brim.*
DOORMAN: I'll see she gets it, sir.

23. INT. OFFICE SUITE. DAY.
SUSAN, *bearing a tray with a cup of coffee and a small
plate of cookies, coming down the corridor of a posh*

medium-tech office suite. OTHER WORKERS *are putting on their coats.*

ANOTHER SECRETARY: *(Passing her)* What you doing on the Weekend, Susan?

SUSAN: Far's I know I'm working here . . . *(She calls to another.)* . . . see you Monday!

24. INT. OFFICE. DAY.

ROSS, *in shirtsleeves, at a desk in a small, spare office.* LANG *sitting across from him, papers strewn in front of them. A red-bound volume as part of the papers.*

LANG: . . . compensation as the discoverer, and head of the design team. Your compensation should be a minimum of . . .

ROSS: . . . every time I *broach* it . . .

LANG: . . . what does he say?

ROSS: . . . he says, "Wait until the Stockholders' Meeting . . ."

LANG: *(Nods)* Well, of course, by then it'll be too late . . . *Sound of an electric bell. They both look up to see* SUSAN *through a window leading into the corridor. She holds the coffee tray.*

LANG: Don't give up. We're going to talk it out. What're you doing tonight?

ROSS: I think I'm going out for dinner.

LANG: Big date . . . ?

ROSS: Some people I met.

LANG: *(Glancing at* SUSAN*)* . . . you giving her a tumble?

ROSS: Well, I perhaps have my sights on different things.

LANG *nods.* ROSS *buzzes the door, and* SUSAN *enters.*

SUSAN: Teatime.

ROSS: Shouldn't you be going home?

SUSAN: Well, yes, I have a hot date for the weekend with

this rich and dishy guy who's going to whisk me to
Connecticut, and we'll loll around in an old Four-
Poster Bed and eat lots of good stuff and so on, but
it's only in my imagination, so here I am.

ROSS: *(Of the coffee, etc.)* Thank you.

SUSAN: You studying Tennis.

ROSS: *(Smiles)* Well, they didn't play in my neighborhood,
when I was a kid.

SUSAN: . . . getting used to the Ways of the Rich . . . ?

ROSS *rises and moves to a wall safe, taking the red-bound
volume.*

LANG: . . . why should he be doing that . . . ?

SUSAN: Oh, come *on* . . .

LANG *gestures to* ROSS, *who nods.*

ROSS: *(To* SUSAN*)* . . . would you turn away, please . . . ?
*She does so. He punches several digits into the keypad of
the wall safe, and a light glows green. He reaches inside
the neck of his shirt, extracts a key on a chain, turns the
key in the lock, and opens the safe. Inside we see a volume, bound in red. He puts two yellow boxes into the
wall safe. He takes out the red-bound volume, takes a pen
from his pocket, makes a notation on it, replaces it, and
locks the safe.*

SUSAN: No, I don't mean to pry. I am just here to serve.

LANG: *(Exiting)* G'night, Joe, Susan . . . *(To* ROSS*)* You get
freed up tonight, gimme a call. Y'know what, I
should stay home, *anyway,* I'm coming down with
something. The Flu . . .

ROSS *puts the key on a chain around his neck, back
down his shirtfront.*

SUSAN: . . . lot of it going around.

Pause.

ROSS *looks at* SUSAN, *as if to say, "Was there anything
else . . . ?"*

SUSAN: When you own the company, can I be Queen?

ROSS: . . . what are you talking about?

SUSAN: Little pitchers have Big Ears.

ROSS: Do they, indeed?

SUSAN: That's their identifying mark.

Pause.

ROSS: . . . what do Loose Lips sink?

Pause.

SUSAN: Ships?

ROSS: . . . see you on Monday, Susan.

SUSAN: Mm. Have a good Weekend, Mr. R . . . *(She starts to exit.)* Oh! 'N I get my *film* back from the Fotomat, you're gonna see, that that guy was *not* on that yacht. 'N you'll owe me a dollar.

He nods. She buzzes her way out of the office. ROSS *picks up the torn book from his desk drawer, looks at it, looks at his watch. He shrugs, picks up the phone, dials.*

ROSS: *(Into the phone)* Yes, in Manhattan. On Central Park West. A Mrs. Initial A. DaSilva . . .

Pause.

He picks up and looks at the torn tennis book.

OPERATOR: *(VO)* I'm sorry, at the Customer's Request, that number is unlisted . . .

25. INT. OFFICE SUITE. DAY.

ROSS, *in his sport coat, carrying various files, leaving a deserted office suite. He passes by a corner office, and* KLEIN *is standing, looking out of the window.*

ROSS: Good night, Mr. Klein . . .

KLEIN *turns, nods.*

KLEIN: *(Of the documents* ROSS *carries)* You're not taking home anything "sensitive," Joe . . . ?

ROSS *comes into the room and closes the door behind him.*

ROSS: Mr. Klein. The Process is in the safe. On noncopyable paper, there are, that I know of, *two* keys, and . . . *(He displays the key on the chain around his neck.)*

KLEIN *nods,* "*Yes, yes, I suppose I'm just over-wrought . . .*" KLEIN *shakes his head, meaning,* "*I don't want to indulge myself.*" ROSS *helps him into his coat, and camera follows them out of the office, past a receptionist station.*

KLEIN: *(To* RECEPTIONIST*)* I'm going home. Tell Susan I'll
    see her on Monday . . .

ROSS: *(To* RECEPTIONIST, *as* KLEIN *moves on ahead, to the*
    elevators) . . . anyone calls, I'll be at home . . .

He hurries to catch up with KLEIN.

26. INT. ELEVATOR. DAY.

The TWO MEN. *Hold, then*

ROSS: Mr. Klein, could I say something to you?

KLEIN: Please, what is it?

ROSS: Forgive me, but your concern with Security, sir. Indi-
    cates that you think someone is going to Take Advan-
    tage of you, sir. *I* don't want to Take Advantage of
    you, and, frankly, I don't want anyone to Take
    Advantage of *Me* . . .

KLEIN: No, I don't understand . . .

27. ANGLE. INT. PARKING GARAGE. DAY.

The TWO *emerge and walk to a waiting green Mercedes limo, whose* DRIVER *is holding open the back door.* KLEIN *and* ROSS *stop.*

ROSS: I would like . . . I would like consideration, sir, for
    the work . . . for the work I have done on the Process,
    and for the wealth I have brought into the
    Company . . .

KLEIN: . . . and I keep *telling* you, son: *everybody* appreci-
ates the work you have done, and you will *find* it rec-
ognized at the Stockholders' . . .
The phone in the car rings, and KLEIN *moves past* ROSS.
KLEIN: *(Exiting, into the car)* I take your point. Let's all do
our jobs, and I'm sure we'll be rewarded, according
to our Just deserts . . .
He closes the car door. The car drives off.

28. ANGLE.
*Cars in the parking garage: several top-of-the-line Mer-
cedeses, a Jaguar, a Ferrari. Pull back to show* ROSS, *trudg-
ing down the line. He gets to a five-year-old, battered
Toyota, opens it, and throws his briefcase inside.*

INT. ROSS'S APARTMENT. NIGHT.
A large calendar sheet, reading, "Friday, March 14."
ROSS, *sitting by the phone, in a suit and tie. He looks at
the phone; he looks at his watch. He takes out a cigar,
reaches for a match, lights the cigar, takes off the jacket,
sighs, turns on the television.*

DISSOLVE TO:

29. INT. ROSS'S APARTMENT. DAY.

ANGLE, INS.
*The matchbook, marked, "Barclay House. Jamaica." The
end of a Cuban cigar in the ashtray. A cup of coffee comes
into the shot. Pull back to show the kitchen table, several
sheets covered in figures,* ROSS, *in blue jeans and T-shirt,
sitting at the table, figuring. He yawns, gets up, looks
down at the papers, gulps his coffee.*

30. EXT. BROADWAY, NEW YORK. DAY.

Ext. Zabar's food store, two JAPANESE MEN, *taking photos of each other in front of the store.* ROSS *comes through the two, carrying a small shopping bag. He starts down the street. He stops, seeing something. He does a double take.*

ANGLE, ROSS'S POV.

Across Columbus Avenue, on a side street, a limousine. A DRIVER *has just opened the back door, and we see a man's back passing across the sidewalk and into a store.*

ANGLE.

ROSS, *moving across the street, curiously.*

ANGLE, ROSS'S POV.

The window of a very posh gun store, full of shotguns and pricy shooting apparel.

ANGLE.

ROSS, *carrying his groceries, coming up to peek in the window. Behind him we see the chauffeured limo and the* DRIVER, *standing by.*

ANGLE, ROSS'S POV.

Through the window, the back of the MAN *who got out of the limo, discussing a shotgun with a* CLERK.

31. ANGLE. INT. THE GUN STORE. DAY.

ROSS *enters, holding his groceries. He is approached by a supercilious* SALESMAN.

SALESMAN: . . . may I help you, sir . . . ?

ROSS *moves past him to the counter, where the* LIMO FEL-LOW *and the* GUN SALESMAN *are discussing a shotgun the*

LIMO FELLOW *holds. As he speaks we see it is* JIMMY, *who
is concluding his confab with the* SALESMAN.
JIMMY: . . . get the balance *perfect* . . .
GUN SALESMAN: . . . of course, Mr. Dell . . .
JIMMY: . . . because when it comes *up* . . .
The GUN SALESMAN *is reaching to* ROSS, *a "May I help
you" expression on his face.* JIMMY *turns and sees* ROSS.
  Beat.
ROSS: Hello.
Pause.
JIMMY: Hello.
Pause.
GUN SALESMAN: Mr. Dell, can I . . .
JIMMY *nods, "It's alright." He looks at* ROSS, *as if to say,
"Was there anything you wanted?"*
ROSS: Well. I guess I'd better get out of your way.
He makes his exit from the store.

32. ANGLE.
On the street, ROSS, *coming out of the store, shaking his
head. He walks away from the shop, the limo behind him.
He gets to the corner and waits for the light to change. He
looks back.* JIMMY *is coming out of the store, the* GUN
SALESMAN *bowing him out.* ROSS *changes his mind and
walks back.*

ANGLE.
JIMMY, *getting into the car, is looking at the* JAPANESE *with
cameras.*
JIMMY: *(To his* LIMO DRIVER*)* Someone should do a book.
  Japanese, all over the World, Front of the World's
  Greatest Monuments . . . taking *pictures* of each
  other . . .

The LIMO DRIVER *senses someone approaching and inter-poses himself between* ROSS, *who is just walking back into the shot, and* JIMMY. JIMMY *motions the* LIMO DRIVER *that it is alright. He looks at* ROSS *to say, "Yes, may I help you . . . ?"*

ROSS: We were supposed to have *dinner* last night. *(Pause)* What happened? Aren't the Laws of Courtesy for the Rich . . . ?

JIMMY: Well, you know, you're a *hell* of a one to talk about courtesy. *(Starts to get in car)*

ROSS: I don't understand.

JIMMY *hesitates.*

JIMMY: Well, you had my sister waiting for you all after-noon.

Pause.

ROSS: What?

JIMMY: What do you mean, "What?"

ROSS: I mean I don't know what you're talking about.

JIMMY: *(Pause)* You were going to bring her the book.

ROSS: I *did* bring her the book.

JIMMY: You *left* it for her. *(Pause)* You told . . . you told me you were going to bring the book to her. I, I called . . . she was *waiting* for you . . . all . . .

ROSS: . . . she was waiting for mmm——— . . . I never said I was going to bring the book . . .

JIMMY: Well, I believe that's what we settled on.

ROSS: It certainly was nnn——— . . . look, look, I didn't . . . Look: I didn't want to *intrude* . . . why would I want to intrude? *My* understanding was that you asked me to drop it *off.*

JIMMY: *(Shakes his head)* . . . that's not what we said.

ROSS: *(As* JIMMY *starts to get into the car)* Well, look here, it certainly *is.* And whatever the thing is with you, I don't appreciate getting accused of a lack of courtesy.

Seriously. *(Pause)* And isn't it possible you misremembered . . .

Pause. JIMMY *hesitates.*

ROSS: Don't look at me like I want something from you. *I* don't want anything from you. You asked *me* to dinner . . . is it possible *you* got it wrong? *(Pause)* Is it possible?

Pause.

JIMMY: It's possible.

ROSS: Alright. That's all I want to say. *(Pause) Thank* you.

Beat.

ROSS *walks away.*

33. INT. ROSS'S APARTMENT. DAY.
ROSS, *in jeans and sweater, working at the figures on his desk. He looks out the window and stops, spotting something.*

33A. ANGLE, ROSS'S POV.
SUSAN, *walking down the street. She holds a small, white paper bag. She looks around and starts up to the door to his building.*

34. ANGLE.
The hall of ROSS's *building. He goes to the door and opens it, and* SUSAN *is there, looking very fetching and casual.*

SUSAN: *(Of bag)* I brought you something *(She hands him the bag.) aaand* I was just in the neighborhood, and thought I would drop in.

35. INT. ROSS'S APARTMENT. DAY. ANGLE, INS.
A plate, the white bag, with a picture of a stylized sun on it, and the logo "Sunshine Bakery." ROSS's *hands take several bagels out of the bag and put them on the plate.*

SUSAN: *(VO)* And, so, as I said, I was just accidentally in
the vicinity, and aren't you courteous and all.

ANGLE.
ROSS *sits down at the kitchen table, across from* SUSAN.
SUSAN: Yes. Well. *(Pause. She takes a bite of a bagel.)*
Good. Make 'em right by my house. Right under my
house. Small world, huh?
Pause.

ROSS *takes an old sheath knife from the knife holder. It
has the figure of a Boy Scout carved into the handle and,
on the reverse, the logo "Be Prepared." He uses it to start
cutting a bagel.*
SUSAN: Nice knife.
ROSS: Got it at the Boy Scouts.
SUSAN: Hell of an organization.
The teakettle begins whistling.
ROSS: . . . a cup of tea . . . ?
SUSAN: No, thank you, no, I'm fine.
He goes to make the tea. And she launches into her speech.
SUSAN: Ever get the urge to do something "adventurous"?
Um. In spite of the ancient wisdom against Interoffice
Romances . . . ?
Camera brings ROSS *back to his seat, where he sips his tea.
He picks up the Sunshine Bakery bag and looks at it, for
something to do.*
SUSAN: Look: Hey, look: Here's the thing: You . . . um . . .
I *know* that you're in line for, for, for Higher Things.
You got it written all over you. But, but . . . but . . .
but you never get anything in life if you don't speak
out for it. *(Pause)* So I wanted to say: I, I'm a hell of a
person. I'm Loyal and True, and I'm not too hard to
look at, and I think you're wonderful, and . . .

(Pause) You know, life is so short. And there're so
   few people you meet . . .
Pause.
ROSS *clears his throat nervously.*
SUSAN: . . . so few people you meet who . . . perhaps you
   think I'm, I'm not, not of your "class," uh . . .
ROSS: Look, Susan, I . . .
She picks up the knife.

ANGLE, INS.
She holds the knife to the camera.

ANGLE. SUSAN.
SUSAN: 'D you like the Boy Scouts?
ROSS: Yes. I did. Learned a lot of things.
SUSAN: *(She nods.)* You're still a Boy Scout today. Aren't
   you?
ROSS: I don't know what you mean.
SUSAN: *(Pause)* You're *good.* *(Pause)* You're . . . you're
   just a Good Nice Guy. *(Pause)* Pretty Rare. Look.
ROSS: . . . Susan . . .
SUSAN: Let *me* be your Good Deed Today. I promise you
   you won't regret it. I promise you, Joe. Listen to me.
   If someone is *drawn* to you . . . if someone is so
   drawn to you . . .
The phone rings. ROSS *moves to the phone.*
SUSAN: You could just Let it Ring, and, you know, we
   could, um . . .
ROSS: *(To phone)* Yes?
JIMMY: *(VO)* Hello? This is Julian Dell. *(Pause)* I'm sorry.
   (Pause) I called to say I'm sorry.
ROSS: *(on phone)* That's alright.
JIMMY: *(VO)* If you're *free* tonight, my sister and I . . .

ANGLE.

ROSS *on the phone.* SUSAN, *looking at him expectantly. He hangs up the phone and turns to her.*

SUSAN: Oh. No. I see. Your Mother's sick, or something, huh . . . ?

ROSS: No. It has to do with work. I have to work, tonight.

SUSAN: *(Nods)* You have to "work" tonight. Huh . . . something with the new . . . ?

ROSS: . . . but it's very lovely to *see* you . . .

She nods to herself, shrugs.

SUSAN: . . . well . . . well. I was in the neighborhood, any-way . . . *(She smiles, picks up her coat. She turns back.)* . . . 'f you ever feel the need of some company . . . or you want someone to cook you "din-ner" . . . or "dinner and breakfast" . . . One Ten Hudson Street, Apartment Five. *(Pause. She starts to exit.)* One Ten Hudson Street. Above a Bakery.

Pause.

ROSS: . . . above a bakery . . .

SUSAN: *(Picks up the bag and toys with it) Above* the *Sun-*shine *Bakery* . . . wouldn't that be just like me . . . *(Pause)* Well . . .

Hold on the Sunshine Bakery logo on the bag. ROSS *takes her to the door and sees her out. We rack focus to the bag and hear the sound of the door being bolted, then of water being turned on in the tub.*

36. INT. ELEVATOR, POSH APARTMENT BUILDING. NIGHT.

ROSS, *in a suit. Elevator stops. Doors open on the* BODY-GUARD *type we saw on the launch standing in a large, loft-like living space. A* BUTLER *nods* ROSS *into the space. Bare white walls, several pieces of modern art, a low sofa, a French Provincial table with a computer on it, a lovely view of Manhattan.* ROSS *moves to the view. He looks down at the table; on it is a photo of a stunning woman in her midtwenties, holding a tennis racket, happy, obviously just having played.* ROSS *picks up the photograph.*

Sound of a door opening. ROSS *looks up.* JIMMY *enters, wearing jeans and a sweatshirt.*

JIMMY: Hi. I'll throw on some things and we'll . . . d'you want a drink . . . ?

He motions to the BUTLER, *who nods and moves off.*

JIMMY *comes and sits next to* ROSS, *perching on the table. He motions, "Excuse me . . . ," and types several things into the computer.*

JIMMY: . . . gotta catch 'em 'fore they close . . .

ROSS: Listen, I wanted to apologize. It's possible *I* misremembered what we . . .

JIMMY *motions for him to stop.*

JIMMY: No, it was me, I'm sure it was my fault, and it *was* my fault, and I'm going to tell you why. *(He motions to the photograph.)* . . . wanna hear a sad story? My sister 'n' I—since we were kids, all that we had was Each Other. *(Pause)* It's *still* all we have. *(Pause)* I . . . um . . . I *called* her, and told her I wanted her to meet a . . . do you know what? *Forget* about it.

The BUTLER *emerges with a tray and two drinks.*

JIMMY: Eh? *Who're* you calling a Crybaby . . .

They drink. JIMMY's *eye is drawn to the computer, and he makes an entry.*

JIMMY: But, Lord, didn't *you* get hot today!

ROSS: *(Smiles)* Got on my High Horse, eh . . . ?

JIMMY: I suppose you *did* . . . got a little bit "ahead" of yourself . . . going on about "you Rich . . ." *(He shakes his head.)* . . . "you" rich . . . ?

ROSS: Did I say that . . . ?

JIMMY: . . . "*You* Rich . . ."

ROSS: Well, you know, I . . . aha. Before you throw me at your little *sister,* I think I should correct a misimpression.

JIMMY: Listening.

ROSS: I'm just a Working Man.

JIMMY: What's a working man doing at the Barclay House. You a Jewel Thief?

ROSS: My company brought me down.

JIMMY: Sell a Million Widgets or something . . . ?

ROSS: Something like that.

JIMMY: "Just a Working Man." That your Dark Secret?

ROSS: That's right.

JIMMY: Well, then that explains it.

ROSS: Explains What?

JIMMY: Your Good Manners.

ROSS: Noble Savage.

JIMMY: Noble Savage. Not even *one* Swiss Bank Account?

ROSS: Wouldn't even know how to open one.

JIMMY: *(Raises a finger)* 'D you have a dog when you were young?

ROSS: Yup, had a dog.

JIMMY: What was his name . . . ?

ROSS: *Paddy.*

JIMMY: *(Types into the computer terminal)* You now have a Swiss Bank Account. Anybody asks you. Credit Suisse de Lausanne, Code Word "Paddy."

ROSS: *(Laughs)* You just opened me a bank account . . . ?

JIMMY: Yeah.

ROSS: Why?

JIMMY: Lavish, awkward gesture. All of fifteen Swiss Francs in it. *But,* you ever want to *impress* anybody . . . they can find out that you have a Swiss Account, but the Swiss Laws prohibit the bank from revealing your Balance. Thus are All Men Made

Equal. *(He turns off the computer. He walks to a door.)* Let me change, and let's meet the little sister.

37. EXT. RESTAURANT. NIGHT.
ROSS *and* JIMMY, *both in suits, getting out of the limo, as the* DRIVER *holds open the door. They enter what seems to be a residential building. They are greeted by a woman,* MAÎTRESSE D'HÔTEL.

MAÎTRESSE D'HÔTEL: Good evening, Mr. Dell . . . you had a message . . . from Mrs. DaSilva.

She hands him a small envelope, which he opens. He looks up to ROSS.

JIMMY: Well, she ain't feeling well. Sends her regrets. Can She Meet us Tomorrow, for Tennis . . . ? You free?

ROSS: Certainly. I hope it's nothing . . .

JIMMY *raises his hand—don't disturb yourself.*

JIMMY: Would you call Mrs. DaSilva's line please, Jane. Tell her tennis tomorrow would be fine. *(To* ROSS*)* Two o'clock? *(*ROSS *nods.)* Take two and call me in the morn——

A tuxedoed MAÎTRE D' *comes up to them.*

MAÎTRE D': Good evening, Mr. Dell.

JIMMY: Hello, George, what's good tonight . . . ?

MAÎTRE D': *(As if at an old joke, or an old routine)* It's *all* good, Mr. Dell.

JIMMY: What'd *you* have?

MAÎTRE D': *(Smiles)* I had the venison.

JIMMY: *Venison.* I was hoping you'd say that. *(To* ROSS*)* In for a *treat* . . .

They start to move past the MAÎTRE D'. *The* MAÎTRE D' *looks a bit distraught.*

JIMMY: 'D is it . . . ? *(Pause)*

MAÎTRE D': It's Members Only tonight, Mr. Dell.

JIMMY: Well, forget about it. Big deal.

MAÎTRE D': . . . it's the board meeting after the meal, and . . .

ROSS: . . . that's fine, let's go somewhere el——

JIMMY: Oh, *Lord* have Mercy, *who* do you have to *know* in this town . . . *(To* MAÎTRE D'*)* You sending me out for a *burger* . . . ?

MAÎTRE D': Mr. Dell, if there were any . . .

JIMMY: No, I know. No, No, Saturday Night, "Members Only . . ." Well . . . *hell* . . . gimme a membership form.

Beat.

The MAÎTRE D' *nods and retreats into a cubicle.*

ROSS: Jimmy, seriously, you don't have to go to all this . . .

JIMMY: It's my Nature, Lad, I'm a Problem Solver with a Heart of . . . *speaking* of Gold . . . *(He is handed a form by the* MAÎTRE D'. *Of form) Look* at this . . . got more *gold* on it than . . . *(He flourishes the form at* ROSS. *We see it is very ornate.)* . . . we aren't electing him "Pope," or anything, we are . . .

ROSS: Really, I . . .

JIMMY: Oh, hell, just *sign* it, and let's, *What* is the phrase . . . ? "Chow down." . . . just *sign* the damn thing . . .

ANGLE, INS.

The very elaborate form is put down, JIMMY's *hands hold it still, and* ROSS *signs it.*

ANGLE.

The form is handed back to the MAÎTRE D', *who glances at it and leads them across the hall toward the restaurant.*

MAÎTRE D': *(As he holds open the door)* Welcome to the club, Mr. Ross.

38. INT. RESTAURANT. NIGHT.

ROSS *and* JIMMY *over brandy.*

ROSS: What do I owe you for the Membership?

JIMMY: D'you know what, *Forget* about it. Pay me when your Ship comes in.

ROSS: Well, do you know what—that may be "presently."

JIMMY: Glad to hear it! Get a tip onna horse?

ROSS: *(Smiles)* The widgets— We're about to bring out a new . . .

JIMMY: . . . Put it in the Bank. Buy AT and T, and do the American Thing.

ROSS: What's that?

JIMMY: Marry a Rich Widow.

ROSS: We used to say, "A nymphomaniac who owns a Liquor Store."

JIMMY: Well, that's right. Money isn't everything.

ROSS: That's what my boss says.

JIMMY: Does he?

ROSS: That's right.

JIMMY: It's like a New Word. Never heard the word before, then, all of a sudden, you hear it three times in one day. "Money isn't Everything" . . . *(Pause)* You see? This is what got my Sister. *(Pause)* You spend your life being told to protect yourself against *fortune* hunters . . . and so you *reject* everyone. And the only ones with the wiles to bypass your defenses are the fortune hunters. *(Pause)* And she married a swine.

He throws up his hands, as if to say, "Well, that's over, and why dwell on unpleasantness . . . ?"

ROSS: Well, I think you have to separate *business,* and *personal* life.

JIMMY: One thing my father taught me about business: do business as if each person you do business with is

trying to screw you, because most likely they are. And
if they're not, you can be pleasantly surprised. You
run your *personal* life that way . . .

ROSS: *(Laughs)* . . . my father knew about business . . .
"Work hard—take all the overtime you can get."

JIMMY: You liked your father, eh?

ROSS: I loved my father.

JIMMY: What'd he do?

ROSS: Worked like a dog, all his life.

JIMMY: Well, he left you a hell of a legacy. *(He yawns,
looks at his watch.)* I'm sure he'd be proud of you.
I'm sure he would.

ROSS: How can you say that?

JIMMY: *(Pause)* People aren't that complicated, Joe. Good
people, bad people . . . they generally look like what
they are.

ROSS: Is that so?

JIMMY: It is.

ROSS: Then why are so many people having such diffi-
culty?

JIMMY: That is the question baffles me . . . play some tennis tomorrow . . .

ROSS: Two o'clock.

39. INT. MIDTOWN TENNIS COURTS. DAY.
ROSS *bouncing a tennis ball off the wall of a deserted
court. He looks up as* JIMMY *approaches. Both wear tennis togs.*

JIMMY: I'm sorry, I'm sorry, I get your . . . *(A phone
rings.* JIMMY *takes a pocket phone out and speaks
into it.)* Yes? Transfer it from the A account and . . .
well, then, take it from the . . . that's right . . . thank
you . . . then . . . *(To* ROSS*)* What've you done with
her . . . ?

ROSS *smiles, shrugs.*

JIMMY: *(Shrugs. Into phone)* Then . . . no. Close out the account, that's alright, just close it out, and put it in the . . . that's right. Put it in the Channel Islands Liquid . . . thank you . . . no, no, get it in writing. Get it in, I don't *care* what the Legal Department said about verbal agr——— . . . you tell them I said to Write it Down. Who gets to do what to who. Thank you . . . *(He hangs up.)* Where's a girl . . . ? *(Checks his watch)*

ROSS: I thought *you* had her . . .

JIMMY: *(Of the phone)* You know what Sam Goldwyn said about Verbal Agreements. Verbal Agreements aren't worth the paper they're printed on.

ROSS: That's what my boss just said to me.

JIMMY: In re: what?

ROSS: I've got this, well, I have a new . . . I *did* something for the Company. And . . . they owe me something. I think I need to "get it in writing."

JIMMY: *I* would. What do they owe you?

ROSS: I think they owe me a lot of money.

JIMMY: What do you mean, "You think"?

ROSS: I invented . . . I invented something for them, it's . . .

Both men's attention is drawn to a WOMAN *who comes out of a locker room. She turns, and* JIMMY *indicates it is not his sister.*

   Pause.

   JIMMY *looks at his watch, takes out his phone, and begins to dial.*

ROSS: It's a "work for hire," they "own" it, but . . .

JIMMY: *(Into phone)* Hello, is Mrs. DaSilva in . . . ? *(To* ROSS) Who told you it was a Work for Hire . . . ?

ROSS: Well . . . *they* did . . . I . . .

JIMMY: You invented it?

ROSS: Yes, I and a . . . I'm sure it belongs to them, I was in their *employ*, and . . .

JIMMY: *(Into the phone)* No, it is her *Brother* . . . who am I speaking to . . . ? *(To ROSS)* There's no reason you should be that sure. You may very well have a proprietary interest in this . . . *what* is it . . . ? *(To phone. He conducts a conversation in some foreign language, then hangs up. To ROSS)* She has the *flu*. *(Pause)* She has the flu. *(Pause)* I'm sorry . . . you were saying? *I* was saying: don't wish it away. You have any questions about the, uh . . . Know What You Own. You have a contract with this company?

ROSS: I do.

JIMMY: Take it to a lawyer. And to a lawyer who specializes in copyright and contract law.

ROSS: I have a friend who's a lawyer . . . he works for the company, he . . .

JIMMY: What's his name?

ROSS: George Lang . . . he works for the company . . .

JIMMY: *(Smiles)* Due respect for Mr. Lang, but, if I may . . . what you want . . . you want an independent view . . . I'd be glad to . . .

ROSS: Um. Look, look, I appreciate it. Please don't take it personally, but I . . . um . . .

JIMMY: . . . the phrase is, "Don't want to mix Business and Pleasure."

ROSS: No no, that's not it. I don't know that I want to adopt an adversary position toward the Company . . .

JIMMY: . . . but you are in an adversarial position.

ROSS: No, no, I think you're wrong . . .

JIMMY: I think you'll find, if what you've done for them is valuable, as you say it is, that if they are indebted to you morally, but not *legally*, *my* experience is that

they will begin to act *cruelly* toward you, to assuage
their guilt.

Pause.

ROSS: How's your sister?

JIMMY: Alright, but if you need some help, ask for it. She's
sick, by the way. Down with the Flu.

ROSS: A lot of it going around.

JIMMY: . . . want to hit some balls . . . ?

40. INT. OFFICE SUITE. DAY.

ROSS, *arriving in the office, passes through the reception
area.* PEOPLE *exchanging "good mornings" as he passes
the* RECEPTIONIST.

RECEPTIONIST: Oh, Mr. Ross, a Mr. Julian *Dell* called for
you . . .

KLEIN *sticks his head out of his office and calls to*
ROSS.

KLEIN: Joe, could you come in here a moment, please . . .

RECEPTIONIST: . . . no message, he said he would call back
lll——

KLEIN: . . . Joe . . . ?

ROSS *motions, "One moment."*

ROSS: *(To* RECEPTIONIST*)* Thank you . . . Oh. Could you
please arrange to have some *flowers* sent for me . . . ?

RECEPTIONIST: On company business . . . ?

ROSS: No, for me personally. To a Mrs. Anna DaSilva, at
the San Remo: I am most s——

SUSAN *appears, coming down the corridor with a file in
her arms.*

SUSAN: *(As she stops at the receptionist desk)* Good morning, Mr. Ross, I . . .

RECEPTIONIST: *(To* ROSS*)* . . . the card . . . ?

He motions to her, "Never mind."

ROSS: I'll get back to it later.

KLEIN: *(From his office)* . . . Joe . . . ?

SUSAN: *(As* ROSS *enters* KLEIN's *office)* Aha! Captured it with my trusty camera! *(She holds her camera up.)* I got my photos back, and I have something to . . .

ROSS *nods, "Yes, yes, yes," and proceeds to* KLEIN's *office.*

ROSS: *(Over his shoulder, to the* RECEPTIONIST*)* . . . thank you, I'll do that later.

41. INT. KLEIN'S OFFICE. DAY.

KLEIN, TWO CORPORATE LAWYER TYPES, *and* ROSS, *some papers arrayed in front of them, on a coffee table.*

LAWYER TYPE: . . . revalidation of your agreement with the Company.

ROSS: No, I don't understand. Why would I have to "revalidate" my agreement?

SECOND LAWYER TYPE: It's purely a formality.

LAWYER TYPE: Before any announcements, before . . .

KLEIN: They're concerned that the Process, Joe . . .

Pause.

ROSS: . . . yes . . . ?

KLEIN: That any uncertainty about . . . about . . .

LAWYER TYPE: About *any* outstanding . . .

SECOND LAWYER TYPE: Look, there are several questions involved here.

ROSS: . . . yes?

SECOND LAWYER TYPE: Questions of *security* . . .

KLEIN *walks to the window, exchanges a look with* ROSS, *meaning, "What can you expect . . . ?"*

ROSS: There's no question of security. There is *one* copy of the Process, it is in . . .

SECOND LAWYER TYPE: . . . any *leakages* of information . . . we have a proprietary Process worth over Half a . . .

ROSS: Well, that's a legitimate concern, but I don't see why
    that means I should sign your . . . what do you call
    it . . . ? "Revalidate" my . . .

LAWYER TYPE: Mr. Ross . . .

ROSS: I'll tell you what I *will* do. *(He picks up the agree-
    ment.)* I will be glad to show this to my lawyer, and
    then respond to you, and thank you for your time.

He gets up and starts to leave the office.

LAWYER TYPE: Mr. Ross, if I may. I don't see any reason for
    you to adopt an attitude which . . .

ROSS: . . . thank you for your time.

ROSS *starts out of the office.* ONE OF THE LAWYERS *closes
the door.*

LAWYER TYPE: . . . these are legitimate concerns of the
    Company, Mr. Ross, and, if I may, your "attitude . . ."

ROSS: My attitude, my attitude, what attitude was that?
    Did you question my attitude when we developed the
    Process, did . . .

KLEIN: . . . can we all calm down . . .

ROSS: No, wait a second, no, wait a second, no, wait a sec-
    ond . . . we *were* calm, all of a sudden, Mr. Klein,
    you're in here with your *lawyers* . . .

KLEIN: All I . . .

ROSS: . . . all *I*, all that I am saying is I plan to take steps to
    insure that I, that I receive . . . I ask you for assur-
    ances, and all I get is you want me to void my con-
    tract, I'm going to make sure . . .

SECOND LAWYER TYPE: . . . what are you talking about,
    Mr. Ross, you aren't talking about, I hope you are not
    talking about any method which would injure the
    Company.

Pause.

ROSS: . . . what do you mean?

SECOND LAWYER TYPE: . . . any premature . . . any prema-
    ture or out-of-school dealings with . . .
ROSS: . . . how dare you?
SECOND LAWYER TYPE: . . . because if we were to find . . .
ROSS: *(To* KLEIN*)* How dare you? How can you hire these
    people and hide behind their dirty skirts? How dare
    you, after what I've . . . ?
He barges out of the office.

42.
Past LANG, *who is wrapped up and unwell looking, open-
ing some medicines in a paper bag.*
LANG: . . . I don't feel well.
ROSS: . . . you don't feel half as bad as me.
LANG: Where you going?
ROSS: I'm going to start looking out for myself.
LANG: We have a five o'clock meet——

ANGLE.
At the receptionist station. ROSS *reading the form.*
ROSS: *(To* RECEPTIONIST*)* Did Mr. Dell leave a number,
    please . . . ?
RECEPTIONIST: Yes, sir, he . . .
ROSS: Would you get it for me, please . . . ?
She dials the number.
ROSS: *(On the phone)* Hello. Hello, *Jimmy.* Yes. I would
    very *much* like to meet with the . . . the sort of person
    who we talked about. *(Pause)* You were right. *(Pause)*
    Yes, yes. I would, yes—tonight. Thank . . . thank
    you . . . what? Well, no, we'll, oh, yes, soon as she's
    out of bed. Absolutely. *(Pause)* Tomorrow. Lunch.
    The Plaza.
ROSS *hangs up the phone.*

RECEPTIONIST: The flowers, sir . . . ?

ROSS: Flowers. Oh. Yes. The . . .

SUSAN *strolls down the hall and stops at the receptionist's area.*

SUSAN: Cathy, could you get these out for me, please? *(She hands some papers to the* RECEPTIONIST.)

ROSS: *(To receptionist)* No, forget about it. Thank you.

43. INT. BOOKSHOP. DAY.

The photo/autograph of Don Budge at the French Open, playing tennis. It is being wrapped.

ROSS: *(VO)* One moment.

ANGLE.

ROSS, *at the counter of the bookshop, writing on a card.*

ANGLE, INS.

The card reads:

>   Mrs. DaSilva
>   For your collection. Hope this finds you improved.
>   Looking forward to making your acquaintance.
>   J.R.

44. ANGLE. EXT. CENTRAL PARK. DAY.

ROSS, *walking. A group of* JAPANESE BUSINESSMEN, *taking photos of each other.*

ANGLE.

ROSS, *the wrapped parcel, on the outside of which is written:* "Mrs. A. DaSilva, San Remo Apartments."

ANGLE.

ROSS, *walking through the group of* BUSINESSMEN.

45. ANGLE. EXT. THE SAN REMO. DAY.
An OLD WOMAN *with a walker. She is accompanied by a*
professional COMPANION.
     ROSS *moves past her and into the lobby of the San Remo.*
     A white-gloved DOORMAN *touches his cap.*
DOORMAN: May I help you, sir?
ROSS: I'd like to leave a package, please . . . ?
DOORMAN: Certainly.
In the BG the OLD WOMAN *and the* COMPANION *enter.*
ROSS: For Mrs. DaSilva.
DOORMAN: . . . Mrs. DaSilva . . . oh. *(To the old woman's*
     COMPANION*)* . . . we have a package for Mrs.
     DaSilva.
The COMPANION *takes the package.*
ROSS: *(To the* DOORMAN*)* I'm sorry. A package for Mrs.
     Anna DaSilva *(Pause) Young* Mrs. DaSilva.
     (Pause) . . . the tennis player.
DOORMAN: *(Pause)* This is the only Mrs. DaSilva in the
     build—— . . . this is Mrs. Anna DaSilva, sir . . .
Hold.
     ROSS *looks at the* OLD WOMAN.

DISSOLVE TO:

46. INT. ROSS'S OFFICE. DAY.
ROSS, *hanging up his coat, wearily slumps into the chair.*
As he does so, he hears a buzz and looks up.

ANGLE, ROSS'S POV.
SUSAN *is seen in the window to the corridor.*

ANGLE.
ROSS *sighs and buzzes her in. She comes in holding an*
album and lays it out on his desk.

SUSAN: Well, you see, you see here, you see here, Mr. Ross,
    I believe you owe me a dollar, sir, a . . .

ROSS: *(Distant. Of album)* . . . I'm sorry . . . ? What . . . ?

SUSAN: *(VO. Opening the pages and turning them as she
    speaks)*

ANGLE, INS.

The album, and we see the pictures described.

SUSAN: Here is my Album of My One Day in the Sun.
    Here are some *photos.*

We see the airport concession area, and the YOUNG
WOMAN *with a mole on her cheek, and the* JAPANESE *in the
background.*

SUSAN: Here are some lovely photos of Japanese honey-
    mooners. Here is the *yacht.* Here is my Ticket, good
    for One Free Return Anytime to Island-of-
    Jamaica . . .

We see the card of the FBI agent, PAT MCCUNE, *etc.*

SUSAN: And *here,* as you see, is our Mystery Man . . . in
    his boat, *which,* you see, has nothing to do with the
    yacht.

*We see the launch coming from a direction off to the side
of the yacht.* SUSAN *continues talking.* CU *on* ROSS, *as he
leafs through the pages.*

SUSAN: *(VO)* So you *never* know who anybody is, as I
    have said, so it would *pay* to be a little Careful who
    you . . .

ROSS: *(Sotto)* Oh, migod . . .

ROSS *stares down at the photos.*

ANGLE, INS.

In the photo album a shot of JIMMY, *his back to the camera, and the* PRINCESS. *We see she is a very beautiful
woman with a mole on her cheek.* ROSS's *hands turn back*

the pages to the shot of the GIRL *at the concession stand, and we see it is the same girl.*

ANGLE.

ROSS, *stunned, and* SUSAN *standing by him.*

SUSAN: . . . what is it?

The phone starts to ring.

SUSAN: . . . what is it . . . ?

ROSS *picks up the phone.*

PHONE: *(VO, Woman's voice)* Mr. Ross? One moment, please, for Mr. Dell . . . *(Pause)* Joe? Joe: *Jimmy.*

ROSS: *(On phone)* Hello, Jimmy. Whatever happened to that Princess . . . ?

JIMMY: *(VO)* I don't know who you're talking about, but we flew her back to From Whence She Came.

ROSS: *(On phone)* . . . what do I owe the honor of your call?

JIMMY: *(VO)* The lawyer wants you to bring your contract when you come. We're going to get you straightened out. I got him to stay in town tonight, and . . .

ROSS: *(On phone)* . . . I appreciate it . . .

ROSS: *(On phone. He covers the receiver. To* SUSAN*)* Would you excuse me, please . . . ?

She nods, and exits.

JIMMY: *(VO)* . . . and here's what I think: whatever this *thing* is . . .

ROSS: *(On phone)* The "thing" . . . ?

JIMMY: *(VO)* The thing that you've done for the Company . . . ?

ROSS: *(On phone)* Yes . . . ?

JIMMY: *(VO)* . . . bring a copy of it, too, will you?

ROSS: *(On phone)* . . . a copy of that, too . . . *(He nods to himself.)*

JIMMY: *(VO)* My man wants to go *over* it with you, and

he wants you to *tell* him precisely what your *input
was* . . . in order to assess your potential ownership
of this . . . *(As if to a secretary)* . . . tell him I'll see
him in Berlin on Wednesday . . . *(To* ROSS) So bring it
along.
ROSS *picks up and toys with the torn "Tennis" book.*
ROSS: *(On phone)* Your Sister going to be there?
JIMMY: *(VO)* She's Out for the Count. But thank you for
asking. So, tomorrow. Lunch. The Plaza.
ROSS: *(On phone)* Yes. The Plaza. Right.
JIMMY: *(VO)* And if you're free after work, let's play some
tennis. Oh . . . and bring those plans. Bring 'em with
you.
The other end of the line goes dead.

ANGLE.
ROSS, *at his desk, picks up the torn cover of the "Tennis"
book.*
  Hold on ROSS *at his desk. He hangs up the phone.*

47. INT. CORRIDOR. DAY.
ROSS, *camera following, moves into the office of* LANG,
who is sneezing and putting on his coat. He looks up at
ROSS.
LANG: I have to cancel our . . . you know, all he wanted to
do was to review the legal aspect of "Security" procedures . . . Legal Aspect—"Security Procedures,"
that's why they call them bureaucr—— . . . are you
alright . . . ?
Beat.
  LANG *leaves the office.*

48. ANGLE. INT. CORRIDOR, OFFICE SUITE. DAY.
A tracking shot. Moving past the offices of KLEIN, *where
we see* KLEIN, *at his desk, dictating to* SUSAN.

ANGLE.
ROSS, *moving past the offices. Camera takes him to a sec-*
retary's cubicle. He looks around. He looks down.

ANGLE, INS.
On the desk, SUSAN's *"Jamaica" album.* ROSS's *hands*
open it, leaf through it, take out a card.

49. INT. OFFICE "COFFEE" AREA. DAY.
ROSS, *holding the card, comes into the small area, closes*
the door behind him, lifts the card, and dials a phone.

ANGLE, INS.
The card reads, "Special Agent Pat McCune, Federal
Bureau of Investigation," etc.

ANGLE.
Tight on ROSS, *as he cradles the phone close and speaks*
into it.
WOMAN'S VOICE ON PHONE: *(VO)* Federal Bureau of
    Investigation . . . your call is being recorded . . .
ROSS: *(On phone)* Special Agent Pat McCune, please . . .
WOMAN'S VOICE: *(VO)* I'm sorry, Agent McCune is out of
    the office. May—
ROSS: It's very important. Please, could you connect me.
    Could you tell me how to contact her . . . ? If you
    could . . . ?
WOMAN'S VOICE: *(VO)* One moment . . .
Sound of electronic beeps, static, etc. Then we hear the
voice of the WOMAN FBI AGENT *from Jamaica, on the*
phone, strained by electronic noise.
MCCUNE: *(On phone. VO)* McCune.
ROSS: *(On phone)* My name is Ross. I met you in Jamaica,
    I . . .

MCCUNE: *(VO)* Oh, Christ, you calling me up to hit on me, in the midst of . . .

ROSS: *(Into the phone)* I'm not calling you to *hit* on you—I'm calling you about that fellow off the yacht.

Pause.

MCCUNE: . . . the fellow off the yacht.

ROSS: That's right. *(Pause)* Were you down there looking for him?

MCCUNE: . . . the fellow off the yacht, calls himself Julian Dell.

ROSS: That's right.

MCCUNE: Who are you?

ROSS: My name is Ross, Joseph *Ross* . . .

MCCUNE: Gimme your date of birth . . .

ROSS: . . . what?

MCCUNE: You heard me.

ROSS: December tenth, nineteen sixty.

MCCUNE: This fellow Dell. Are you with him now?

ROSS: No.

Pause.

MCCUNE: Alright. I'm going to give you an address. You meet me there. Do you have a pencil . . . ?

50. EXT. BROOKLYN SEMI-INDUSTRIAL NEIGHBORHOOD. NIGHT.

A cab pulls up in front of a block of old brownstones. ROSS *gets out of the cab, looks around. The cab pulls away.* ROSS *looks down at a sheet of paper in his hand, begins to walk down the street. He turns a corner. He is joined by a* TOUGH-LOOKING FELLOW *in work clothes, who steps out of the shadows.*

TOUGH-LOOKING FELLOW: . . . just keep walking.

ROSS *accompanies the* MAN *to a corner, where he is motioned to stop again. In the BG we see another semi-*

industrial street with a battered red van parked some fifty yards up it. The van side door opens and a PERSON *gets out and begins walking toward* ROSS *and the* MAN. *It is a young* WOMAN *in chinos, a bomber jacket, and a watch cap. They round the corner, she takes off the watch cap, and we see it is the* FBI WOMAN *from Jamaica. They stop under a streetlamp. The woman,* PAT MCCUNE, *takes a sheet of fax paper from her jacket and studies it.*

ROSS: . . . what . . . ?

MCCUNE: *(To* TOUGH-LOOKING FELLOW*)* Following him?

The TOUGH-LOOKING FELLOW *shakes his head.*

ROSS: *(Clears his throat)* . . . my name is . . .

MCCUNE: Well, yeah, no, I know who you are . . . *(She holds the fax paper toward him.)*

ANGLE, INS.

The fax paper bears a facsimile of his driver's license and other pertinent data. It is headed, "FBI, File Use Only," and other hieroglyphics.

MCCUNE: Ross, Joseph A. D.O.B. twelve ten sixty . . .

ANGLE.

The group. They walk and talk, and proceed to a car where the FIRST MAN *gets out.*

MCCUNE: Zat it? What was your mother's maiden name . . . ?

ROSS: . . . Bainbridge.

MCCUNE: What was *her* mother's maiden name . . . ?

She gestures to one of the MEN, *in mime: "I want to take a ride with this fellow, can you stay here and mind the store . . . ?"*

FIRST MAN: *(Into microphone)* . . . sitrep on the Paul? *(He listens.)* Sally for a bit-of-seven . . . ? *(He listens and nods "okay" to* MCCUNE.*)*

ROSS: . . . Laval . . .

MCCUNE *nods, motions to the* SECOND MAN *to drive.*

MCCUNE: *(To* ROSS*)* Get in the car, would you, Mr.
      Ross . . . ?

ROSS *starts to do so. As* MCCUNE *gets into the car, she
speaks, back, to the* FIRST MAN, *gesturing in the direction
of her van.*

MCCUNE: If they move, gimmeashout, and we'll catch you
      rolling . . .

The car starts off.

51. EXT. TRUCKER'S DINER. NIGHT.

A truck stop in the BG. The Elevated. The SECOND FBI
MAN *is in the car, behind him several rigs, and the diner.
He glances toward the diner, stretches, gets up, gets out of
the car, looks around, and puts his hand to his ear, as if
receiving a radio transmission.*

52. INT. DINER. NIGHT.

ANGLE, INS.

*A small, wire-bound notebook, held on the knee. In the
book we see written in a woman's handwriting, "Mrs. A.
DaSilva, San Remo. Julian Dell. Ross meets with Dell at
Midtown Tennis," and several dates and times.*

ROSS: *(VO)* . . . to deliver the plans to him.

MCCUNE: *(Taking notes)* . . . to deliver the plans . . .

ROSS: Yes. The plans . . . are for a project, which . . .

MCCUNE: Hey, don't tell *me*. 'F it's so damn secret, *I* don't
      wanna know . . . *(She closes the notebook.)* 'F our
      friend is after them, I assume they're valuable.

ROSS: . . . they're *very* valuable.

MCCUNE: Alright. *(She sighs.)* How much've you told this
      guy?

ROSS: I haven't told him *anything*.

MCCUNE: . . . how much've you told him?

ROSS: I haven't done anything illegal, my God, that's why
      I . . .

MCCUNE: Has he tried to *bribe* you?

ROSS: Bribe me? *(Pause)* No, he's, he's offered me . . .
      uh . . . uh . . .

MCCUNE: Yeah. You're in a lot of trouble.

ROSS: I haven't done anything wr——

MCCUNE: Not from me, Mr. Ross. . . . But you have an
      advantage, if he doesn't know you know. . . . Whad-
      daya want to do?

ROSS: I don't understand.

MCCUNE: Do you want to help?

Pause.

ROSS: Yes.

MCCUNE: Are you sure?

ROSS: Yes, I'm sure. Why wouldn't I be sure?

MCCUNE: 'F he can't trick you or bribe you, he's going to
      threaten you or hurt you, and it could get dirty.

ROSS: I want to help you catch him.

MCCUNE: . . . hurt your feelings, did he?

ROSS: That's right.

MCCUNE: It's any consolation, you ain't the only one,
      he's . . .

The SECOND FBI MAN *comes into the diner and slides into
the booth.*

FBI MAN: *(Sotto, to* MCCUNE*)* . . . they're rolling.

MCCUNE *nods and starts out of the booth.*

MCCUNE: *(To* ROSS*)* . . . I gotta go to work. *Where's* the
      meet?

ROSS: . . . Plaza. At noon.

MCCUNE: *(As she leaves)* He'll change it. Don't worry. I'll
      be on top of it. Don't worry.

ROSS: How will I contact you?

MCCUNE: We're on top of it—keep your sense of
      humor . . .

53. INT. ROSS'S APARTMENT. DAY.

ANGLE, INS.
*The Boy Scout knife, point stuck in the counter, being
slowly twirled.*

ANGLE.
ROSS, *in shirt and tie, sitting, a cup of coffee before him,
twirling the knife idly.*
    The phone rings. He picks it up.
ROSS: *(To phone)* Hello.
JIMMY: *(VO)* Hello. Joe? Jimmy.
ROSS: Jimmy. How are you?
JIMMY: What'd you go out last night, I was calling you,
      and . . .
ROSS: . . . went to a movie.
JIMMY: . . . what'd you see?
ROSS: . . . I . . .
JIMMY: . . . listen, Joe. Got to change the meeting. The
      lawyer can't do noon.
ROSS: . . . he can't do noon . . .
JIMMY: Make it at ten, can you?
ROSS: . . . ten A.M.
JIMMY: . . . and listen, listen . . . here's what he wants to
      do. Meet us in the park.
ROSS: . . . in the park.
JIMMY: . . . by the carousel.
ROSS: . . . why is that?
JIMMY: He says for secrecy. To protect yourself. The
      carousel, at ten. And bring the Process.

ROSS: . . . bring the Process.

ROSS *hangs up the phone. He toys with the knife for a moment. The phone rings again; he picks it up.*

MAN'S VOICE ON PHONE: *(VO)* . . . we have it. He wanted to meet, the carousel at ten. Do what he says. Do what he says, but meet us at nine-thirty, the Dairy, Central Park. You know it?

ROSS: Ycs.

MAN'S VOICE ON PHONE: *(VO)* Dairy, Central Park. Nine-thirty.

We hear the sound of the other phone being hung up.

ROSS *takes a bagel from the Sunshine Bakery bag. He takes a bite.*

54. EXT. CENTRAL PARK MALL. DAY.

Several JAPANESE TOURISTS *walking the deserted mall.*

ROSS *walking hurriedly, checks his watch. We see it is 9:15. Under* ROSS's *arm is the red-bound "Process."*

ANGLE.

The Central Park Dairy. In the BG an old man in a sanitation outfit picking up trash.

ROSS *walks into the shot. Checks his watch, looks around, buys a bag of popcorn from a* CART VENDOR. *The* SANITATION MAN *walks past him and whispers.*

SANITATION MAN: . . . keeping walking, Mr. Ross. Walk into the men's room.

55. INT. MEN'S ROOM, CENTRAL PARK. DAY.

ROSS *enters the room. There is a* YOUNG MAN *of similar coloring and build, dressed in a similar coat, and, next to him, one of the FBI men from the night before. The* FBI

MAN *takes* ROSS's *popcorn from him, hands it to the* DOU-
BLE, *and nods. The* DOUBLE *waits for a count or two, then
exits the rest room.* ROSS *looks around.* MCCUNE *and a
very fit, fortyish man in a business suit,* KELLY, *are also in
the rest room.*

    Hold.

    The young FBI man, LEVY, *approximately thirty, puts
his hand to his ear, waits.*

KELLY: It's an interesting setup, Mr. Ross. It is the oldest
    confidence game on the books. The Spanish Prisoner.
    'S how far back it goes, the Glory Days of Spain. Fel-
    low says, him and his sister, wealthy refugees, left a
    fortune in the Home Country. He got out, girl and the
    money stuck in Spain. Here is her most beautiful por-
    trait. And he needs money to get her and the fortune
    out. Man who supplies the money gets the fortune
    and the girl. Oldest con in the world. Intelligent
    people—play on their vanity and greed . . . interesting
    twist.

LEVY, *with his hand to his ear, nods.*

LEVY: . . . they went for it.

KELLY: *(To* LEVY*)* How're we doing on *time* . . . ?

LEVY *looks at his watch and shrugs.*

KELLY: Alright, well, let's make haste slowly . . . plug 'em
    in. . . . We're going to have you wear a radio trans-
    mitter. Here is what we need. We need you to *refuse*
    to give him the material . . .

*As they speak, they begin to wire him into a harness,
which holds a transmitter.*

ROSS: . . . to *refuse* . . .

KELLY: You have to refuse. He . . .

ROSS: *(Of the red-bound "Process")* . . . but your man
    told me to bring it.

ROSS *holds up the Process.* KELLY *picks it up and leafs through it, and we see the many pages covered in mathematical notation.*

KELLY: . . . he told you to bring it?

ROSS: He told me to do everything that . . .

KELLY: *(Handing the Process back)* . . . this the Real Thing?

ROSS: Yes.

KELLY: Well. *(To* LEVY, *working on the wire)* How're we doing?

LEVY *nods.*

KELLY: The important thing is to *refuse* to deal with him. He will then either *bribe* or *threaten* you, and we have him on tape, 'n' he's gonna have to answer for it.

ROSS: You've been after him a long time . . .

The AGENTS *look at each other.*

ROSS: . . . that's why you were in Jamaica . . .

KELLY: . . . this is a Very Bad Actor, Mr. Ross. We have been after him some time, and we are very grateful for your help. Would you speak, please . . . ?

ROSS *looks confused, then starts speaking into the microphone.*

KELLY: . . . just speak normally . . .

ROSS: . . . hello . . . hello . . . hello . . .

LEVY: . . . it's time . . .

KELLY: We'll have you in sight all the time . . . we . . .

MCCUNE: . . . can we put a vest on him . . . ?

KELLY: . . . it's going to bulk up . . . *(To* ROSS) There is very little likelihood of physical danger. *Should* it start to break up . . .

MCCUNE: . . . if there's shooting . . .

KELLY: . . . if there's shooting. Stay put. Do Not Move. What did I just tell you . . . ?

ROSS: Do not move.

MCCUNE: . . . it's time to go.

KELLY: . . . we appreciate your help. *(Shakes hands with*
   ROSS*)*

SANITATION MAN: 'S coming back . . .

The group looks up and picks up the pace.

MCCUNE: The transmitter's good for three hours, more
   than enough time, good for twenty-five yards, we'll
   be closer than that.

KELLY: Give 'em a word.

MCCUNE: You get in trouble, just say the word
   happiness . . . say it.

ROSS: Happiness . . .

LEVY *finishes attaching the wire.*

LEVY: . . . all done . . .

KELLY: You *wait,* until he offers you money, *or* he threat-
   ens you . . . and then hand him the package. When
   you hand it to him, you identify what it is . . .

ROSS: . . . I understand . . .

The DOUBLE *for* ROSS *enters the rest room.* ROSS *starts to
leave. He nods. The* YOUNG FBI MAN *starts to talk into his
lapel mike. He nods "okay."* ROSS *starts to leave the rest
room. He is stopped by* MCCUNE, *who takes the popcorn
from the* DOUBLE *and passes it to* ROSS.

56. EXT. THE REST ROOM. DAY.

ROSS, *holding the red-bound Process, walking through the
park. He looks over at the* SANITATION MAN, *who pays no
attention to him.*

ANGLE.

On ROSS, *as he walks. A pair of* JAPANESE TOURISTS *are
taking photos of each other. A* YOUNG MAN *is working on
a disabled bicycle. He looks up at* ROSS.

57. THE CAROUSEL, CENTRAL PARK. DAY.
Two WOMEN *sit chatting on a bench.* ROSS *moves toward
the carousel. He checks his watch and sits down, holding
on to the red-bound Process. The* WOMEN *move off. A
busload of* SCHOOLCHILDREN *arrive, debark, and stand in
line.*

ANGLE, ROSS'S POV.
The TICKET SELLER *at the carousel lowers his head and
talks into a telephone.*

ANGLE.
ROSS, *sitting, holding the Process. He brightens, looking at*
TWO MEN *walking toward him.*

ANGLE, ROSS'S POV.
They veer away. Neither of them is JIMMY DELL.

ANGLE.
ROSS, *sitting on his bench. He lightly touches the appara-
tus under his shirt; he checks his watch. We see the*
SCHOOLCHILDREN *in the BG.*

DISSOLVE TO:

58. THE CAROUSEL, EMPTY AND STILL. DAY.
ROSS, *his shirt collar undone, looks down at his watch. He
rises, and walks to a telephone.*

ANGLE.
ROSS *as he takes a card from his pocket.*

ANGLE, INS.
It is the FBI card of AGENT MCCUNE.

ANGLE.
ROSS *picks up the phone and dials. We hear, "The number you have reached is not in service . . ." ROSS is already picking up the yellow pages from its connection to the telephone post.*

ANGLE, INS.
The listing for Federal Bureau of Investigation.

ANGLE.
ROSS *dials the phone.*
WOMAN'S VOICE: *(On phone)* Federal Bureau of Investigation.
ROSS: *(On phone)* Please, can you patch me through to Special Agent Pat McCune.
WOMAN'S VOICE: *(On phone)* One moment . . .
MAN'S VOICE: *(On phone)* McCune . . .
ROSS: I would like to speak to Special Agent Pat McCune . . .
MAN'S VOICE: *(On phone)* This is Pat McCune . . . how can I help you . . . ?
ROSS *hangs up the phone. He is staring at something.*

ANGLE, ROSS'S POV.
It is the red volume, "The Process."

ANGLE, INS.
ROSS's *hand comes into the shot and opens the cover.*

ANGLE, XCU.
ROSS, *sadly nodding as he looks down.*

ANGLE.
ROSS, *riffling through the book. He looks away. He picks up the FBI card, shreds it, and tosses it on the ground. He looks down.*

ANGLE, INS., ROSS'S POV.
The red book, ROSS's *hand riffling through it. Every page is blank.*

DISSOLVE TO:

59. INT. ELEVATOR. DAY.
ROSS, *standing next to a large* OLDER MAN *in a topcoat.*
  Beat.
ROSS: I couldn't feel like more of a fool . . .
The elevator door opens to reveal several uniformed NYPD OFFICERS, *a* MAN *dusting for fingerprints. It is the floor of* JIMMY'S *luxury apartment; the floor is empty.* ROSS *and the* OLDER MAN *walk into the room. They move toward the door to the bulk of the apartment.*
OLDER MAN: . . . and his living quarters were in *there* . . . ?
He opens the door. It is a large broom closet.
FINGERPRINT TECHNICIAN: . . . absolutely clean, not a
        print anywhere . . .
The OLDER MAN *nods. They proceed toward the elevator.*

ANGLE.
On ROSS, *looking at something.*

60. INT. "CLUB ANTEROOM." DAY.
Angle to show ROSS *looking at the "Office" area of the club. The* OLDER POLICEMAN *and* ASSISTANTS *are talking to a* JANITOR. *They turn back toward* ROSS.
OLDER POLICEMAN: *(Motioning to the "Office" area,*
        which is a coat-check room) . . . a coat-check room,

Mr. Ross . . . *(He gestures across the hall to a closed restaurant.)* . . . it's a restaurant, always has been, never been a private club . . .

61. INT. NYPD INTERROGATION ROOM. DAY.
ROSS, *sitting immobile next to a blank wall at a steel desk.*
SUSAN: *(VO)* . . . the . . . the photos of our trip.
POLICEWOMAN: *(VO)* . . . and this fellow? Getting off the boat?
SUSAN: *(VO)* Well, we joked about that.
POLICEWOMAN: *(VO)* . . . what do you mean?
SUSAN: *(VO)* I said he was never *on* the boat.
POLICEWOMAN: *(VO)* . . . *was* he on the boat . . . ?

ANGLE, ROSS'S POV.
Several POLICE OFFICERS. *Beyond them a two-way mirror and* SUSAN, *in an adjoining room, being questioned by the* POLICEWOMAN. *She has the photo album in front of her.*
SUSAN: Well, I don't know if he was on the boat or not.
    (Pause) I just used it . . . I just used it as an excuse to make conversation.
POLICEWOMEN: . . . to make conversation with Mr. Ross . . .
SUSAN: That's right.
POLICEWOMAN: Why . . . ?
SUSAN: I . . .
Pause.
POLICEWOMAN: Are you having an affair with Mr. Ross . . . ?
SUSAN: What, what's . . .
POLICEWOMAN: *(Looking at the album)* Now do you have any photographs in which we see this other man's face . . . ?

SUSAN: . . . what's the matter, has something happened to
    Mr. Ross . . . ?

DISSOLVE TO:

62. INT. INTERROGATION ROOM. DAY.
ROSS *and the* OFFICERS *in shirtsleeves. Coffee and dough-
nut residue on the previously bare side table. As the inter-
rogation of* ROSS *continues. The FBI "radio wire"
apparatus lies on the table.*
CHIEF INTERROGATOR: . . . this man didn't *offer* you any-
    thing . . .
ROSS: I told you, he . . .
CHIEF INTERROGATOR: *(Checking notes)* You purchased a
    first-class ticket for . . . for Susan Ricci, an employee
    in your office, paid cash, a total of . . .
ROSS: *(Repeating himself)* . . . the money was from Mr.
    Lang . . .
INSPECTOR: George Lang, your colleague . . .
ROSS: He won it at a casino, and told me to . . .
INSPECTOR: . . . to give it to a Charitable Cause . . . ?
ROSS: That's right.
INSPECTOR: And you thought that meant to buy a first-
    class ticket.
Pause.
ROSS: Well. Perhaps . . . perhaps I was . . .
INSPECTOR: . . . you were what?
ROSS: Showing off.
INSPECTOR: Showing off for the girl. *(Pause)* Why?
ROSS: I, I don't know. What, what does it *matter*—it
    wasn't *my* money, it was . . . ask *George* . . .
INSPECTOR: We will. Believe me. He's ill. We'll have him in
    as soon as . . .

An ASSISTANT *draws the attention of the* CHIEF INSPECTOR *to a notation on the list.*

CHIEF INTERROGATOR: . . . bought some clothes down there.

ROSS: . . . that's right.

CHIEF INTERROGATOR: . . . paid cash again . . .

ROSS: I went to the Hotel Office, I changed some *traveler's* checks, and, yes, I paid cash in the clothing store.

CHIEF INTERROGATOR: So Mr. Lang didn't give you that money, too.

ROSS: No.

INSPECTOR: Why'd you change the checks in the Hotel Office? *(Pause)* Why not just use them at the clothes shop? *(Pause)* Why not?

ROSS: . . . I don't know . . .

INSPECTOR: . . . you don't know why you did that.

ROSS: No.

CHIEF INTERROGATOR: . . . spent a lot of money on those clothes.

ROSS: I, uh, I wanted to indulge myself.

CHIEF INTERROGATOR: . . . indulge yourself . . .

ROSS: I did it reluctantly. You can ask Mr. Lang.

CHIEF INTERROGATOR: . . . he's your attorney . . . ?

ROSS: He's *an* attorney, he's an attorney for the *company,* he's my friend, he . . .

INSPECTOR: *(Checks list) Why* isn't he here?

ASSISTANT: He's ill.

CHIEF INTERROGATOR: You checked him out?

INSPECTOR *nods.*

CHIEF INTERROGATOR: And he's gonna clear you of everything . . . ?

ROSS: I've *done* nothing . . .

CHIEF INTERROGATOR: He have special "knowledge" of this case?

ROSS: Yes, he does, and when you *see* him . . .

CHIEF INTERROGATOR: *(Nodding, looks at another piece of paper)* Uh huh. You know, you know, Mr. Ross . . . you're in a lot of trouble . . .

ROSS: I came to *you* . . .

CHIEF INTERROGATOR: . . . and we're the *least* of it. I promise you. You can cooperate and turn back the clock right now, give your employer back what you took, 'f you've still got it . . . and I'll *deal* with you. But if we've got to turn this over . . . *(He shrugs his shoulders.)*

ROSS: . . . what do you mean?

CHIEF INTERROGATOR: The Feds won't deal with you, you know. They'll put you inside for All day.

ROSS: . . . what are you talking about?

CHIEF INTERROGATOR: I'm talking about unreported income.

ROSS: I've explained to you, the first-class ticket . . .

INSPECTOR: *(Gestures at sheet)* . . . got any undisclosed bank accounts?

ROSS: . . . just what you see . . .

INSPECTOR: No Gold, no Foreign Money stashed away . . . ?

ROSS: I'm just a salaried employee . . .

INSPECTOR: No "Swiss Bank Accounts" . . .

ROSS: I've told you, I . . . *(He stops.)*

INSPECTOR: *(Showing him a slip of paper)* You've got an account at the Credit Suisse de Lausanne. Numbered Account. Opened last week.

Pause.

ROSS: There's nothing in that account.

INSPECTOR: Then what's it doing there . . . ?

ROSS: It was a joke, Jimmy said . . .

INSPECTOR: Goddammit man, *won't* you come clean? Don't you know you're *beat*? It's *over*. It's All Done . . .

ROSS: I've *told* you . . . believe me, I . . . look: Look. The fellow is, he's obviously a . . . you must have him in your files. You must have a *record* of him.

CHIEF INTERROGATOR: A record. How would we find such a record? *(Pause)* You want to give us a photograph . . . fingerprints . . . ?

Pause.

ROSS: His fingerprints.

CHIEF INTERROGATOR: You have something with his fingerprints . . . ?

Pause.

ROSS: . . . uh . . .

The SECOND INSPECTOR *gestures, meaning, "Why are we wasting our time?" The* CHIEF INSPECTOR *makes a gesture of acquiescence.*

CHIEF INTERROGATOR: *(Showing a piece of paper)* . . . that your signature . . . ?

ANGLE, INS.

It is the gold-leafed, scrolled "Club" membership.

ANGLE.

ROSS, *looking down at it.*

ROSS: I . . .

ANGLE.

ROSS *and the* CHIEF INTERROGATOR:

CHIEF INTERROGATOR: . . . planning a trip to Venezuela?

ROSS: Why would I go to Venezuela?

CHIEF INTERROGATOR: They have no extradition treaty
　　with the United States.
ROSS: I have no intention of going to Venezuela.

ANGLE, INS.
The CHIEF INTERROGATOR's *hands on the document move,
to reveal it is a request for asylum, to the Venezuelan con-
sulate.*

ANGLE.
ROSS *and the* CHIEF INTERROGATOR.
Pause.
CHIEF INTERROGATOR: Now, Mr. Ross, if I told *you* this
　　story, would you believe it?
ROSS: I want a lawyer.
CHIEF INTERROGATOR: . . . I would say so.

63. INT. NYC JAIL HOLDING TANK. DAY.
ROSS *sitting, hunched up, on a bench. Several* OTHER MEN
in the cell, asleep. One DRUNK *mutters continually,* "St.
Paddy's Day—I'm going to be stuck in the joint on St.
Paddy's Day . . ."
　　Hold.
　　Sound of a metal door opening. ROSS *comes partially
awake. He looks around.*

64. ANGLE.
A JAILER, *leading* ROSS *out, down a jail corridor, into a
side room.*

ANGLE.
Moving POV of ROSS *as he moves past the cells. The door
to the side room opens; in it is sitting* KLEIN.

65. ANGLE.
ROSS, *entering the room, is motioned to a chair. In the room are* KLEIN *and* ONE OF THE LAWYER TYPES *we first saw in* KLEIN's *office.* ROSS *looks around and sits, tentatively.* KLEIN *starts to speak, shakes his head, pauses.*

KLEIN: If . . . I treated you . . . less than well . . . *(Pause)* If . . .

The LAWYER TYPE *starts to interrupt, and* KLEIN *stops him.*
If the Process is *gone* . . . *(Pause)* If . . . we've lost it . . . my, um, my *family* and I . . . *(He shakes his head, to say, "That is not what I want to say.")* I am afraid I brought it on myself, and I want to apologize. If . . . my "actions" *drove* you to this . . .

The LAWYER *starts to interrupt again.*

KLEIN: No, be quiet, and I'm going to finish. *(To* ROSS*)* I'm *asking* you. I'm *pleading* with you . . . however you want to put it. And whatever trouble you may be in, I swear I will help you. *(Pause)* I've paid your bail. Please. *(He hands* ROSS *a card.)* Bring it back to me. Bring it back, and I *swear* to you . . .

LAWYER TYPE: Mr. Klein is acting against my instructions . . . we're giving you until tomorrow night.

KLEIN: *(Imploring)* . . . Bring it Back . . .

66. INT. JAILHOUSE. NIGHT.
A property window, the CLERK, *passing back an envelope with* ROSS's *valuables.*

ROSS: . . . thank you.

CLERK: *(Cheerily)* . . . you'll be back . . .

67. EXT. NYPD STATION HOUSE. NIGHT.
ROSS, *across the street from the Station House, talking on a pay phone. The Station House is in the BG.*

ROSS: . . . need to talk.

LANG: *(VO, on phone)* Joe . . . what the hell is going on . . . ?

ROSS: *(On phone)* George: I need to talk to you. I know you're sick, but . . .

LANG: *(VO, on phone)* No. Come over, but what's . . .

ROSS: *(On phone)* I need to talk to you. . . . Lord . . . I need your help . . . I need your help, and your *advice*, and . . .

LANG: *(VO, on phone)* . . . come right up.

ROSS *hangs up the phone and starts off down the street. He hails a cab; as he does he looks back over his shoulder, and a* PLAINCLOTHES POLICEMAN, *looking at him, gets into his car.*

DISSOLVE TO:

68. EXT. CITY STREET, WEST END AVENUE. NIGHT.
ROSS *entering a building. We see the cop car, across the street, coming to a stop and a* MAN *getting out.*

69. INT. APARTMENT BUILDING CORRIDOR. NIGHT.
ROSS, *getting out of the elevator. He passes a window looking out onto the street and sees, and we see, down below, the* POLICEMAN, *standing by his car, at a streetlight.*

We follow ROSS *down the corridor, around a corner. We hear a shade flapping in the wind.* ROSS *stops.*

ANGLE, ROSS'S POV.
An open door. Beyond, a shade flapping by a back window.

70. ANGLE.
ROSS *enters the apartment, turns. Camera takes him into the apartment. In the bedroom, where* ROSS *stops.*

ANGLE, ROSS'S POV.

LANG, *lying on the bed, dead—the Boy Scout sheath knife stuck in his chest, the bed covered in blood.* ROSS *comes into the shot. He bends down, leans on the bed, looks at the blood. He recoils from the sight of the corpse and leans against the wall. He looks at the wall and the bloody handprint he has left. His gaze moves to the side.*

ANGLE.

Out the window an oblique view of the POLICEMAN *waiting by his car.*

71. EXT. REAR OF APARTMENT BUILDING. NIGHT.

The reverse view of the flapping shade. Camera tilts down to show ROSS, *hurriedly descending the fire escape.*

72. EXT. CITY STREET. NIGHT.

ROSS, *slinking out of an alley, onto Broadway, and down into the subway, as he glances over his shoulder.*

73. INT. SUBWAY STATION. NIGHT. A DESERTED STATION.

ROSS *descends, buys a token. He passes through the toll machine. He looks down and recoils.*

ANGLE, ROSS'S POV, INS.

His hand, covered in blood. He hears another person walking.

ANGLE.

ROSS *turns and hurries away, deeper into the station, thrusting his hand into his pocket. He walks on, turns a corner in the station.*

WOMAN'S VOICE: *(VO)* Murderer!

ANGLE, XCU.
ROSS, *as he slowly turns.*
WOMAN'S VOICE: *(VO, continued)* Murderer!
     Murderer . . . !
ROSS *turns.*

ANGLE, ROSS'S POV.
A WOMAN, *screaming at her husband.*
WOMAN: . . . you thief. You murderer . . . you killed my
     love for you. . . . You call yourself a man. You call
     yourself my *husband* . . .
The WOMAN *continues screaming. In the BG we see* ROSS
slink away.

74. ANGLE.
ROSS *in a transfer area, a sign proclaiming many trains
and lines in different directions. He looks at the signs for
the various lines. He turns, turns back again, unsure
where to go. He sees something.*

ANGLE, ROSS'S POV.
A TRANSIT POLICEMAN, *on his rounds, walking into* ROSS'S
area.

ANGLE.
The POLICEMAN *in the BG,* ROSS *in the foreground, walking casually toward the camera. We hear the sound of a
train approaching.*

75. ANGLE. INT. SUBWAY CAR. NIGHT.
ROSS *sitting in the near-deserted car. He casts his eyes
around distraught. He stops.*

ANGLE. INT. ROSS'S POV.
A sign for the "Sunshine Bakery" with the logo we have seen before of the stylized sun, and an address: 110 *Hudson Street, New York, New York.*

DISSOLVE TO:

76. EXT. SUNSHINE BAKERY, HUDSON STREET. DAWN.
The logo of the stylized sun. Across the street, a JAPANESE MAN *opening up his small convenience store next to it. He is stringing up a green bunting with shamrocks on it.*

77. ANGLE. INT. STAIRCASE OF THE SMALL BUILDING. DAWN.
ROSS, *climbing the staircase. He looks back to see if he is being followed.*

INT. SUSAN'S APARTMENT. DAWN.
SUSAN, *in a bathrobe, looking up at a security TV screen showing* ROSS *climbing her stairs.*

ANGLE.
On the staircase, ROSS *climbing. Sound of a door opening. He looks to see* SUSAN, *above him.*

78. INT. SUSAN'S APARTMENT. DAWN.
SUSAN *closing, locking, and bolting her door. Sound of water running. She looks back.*

ANGLE, ROSS'S POV.
ROSS, *in the bathroom, furiously scrubbing his hands.*

ANGLE.
SUSAN, *looking on, as she moves to her closet and starts to get dressed.* ROSS *still in the BG.*

DISSOLVE TO:

79. INT. SUSAN'S BEDROOM. DAY.
ROSS *sitting on a chair;* SUSAN *sitting cross-legged on the bed. Both hold mugs of coffee.*
Pause.
SUSAN: Well . . .
ROSS: . . . and I think . . . the only way to make sense of it is . . . is perhaps that I *have* done it . . .
SUSAN: . . . but you *haven't* done it . . . what are you talking about?
ROSS: That my *greed* or . . .
He trails off. She shakes her head, starts out of the room. Hold on ROSS. *He sits, then rises and stealthily moves to the door.*

ANGLE.
Walking into his own POV, beyond ROSS, *we see* SUSAN *on the phone. He walks up on her and takes the phone.*
ROSS: What are you *doing* . . . who are you *calling* . . . ?
SUSAN *looks up at him, first startled, then pitying.*
SUSAN: . . . I'm calling in sick . . . *(Pause)* I'm calling in sick . . .
PHONE: *(VO, recorded message)* Please leave your message at the tone. If you know the employee's extension number . . .
SUSAN *punches a number on the phone.*
SUSAN: *(Into phone)* This is Susan Ricci. I have the flu. I won't be in today. *(She hangs up. To* ROSS) You poor sap. *(Pause)* That's why they picked you. Innit?

(Pause) You're the Boy Scout. . . . You're the *inno-cent.* You're the victim.

ROSS: They used me because I was weak.

SUSAN: You can call it whatever you want. But we're going to get out of it. Now, listen.

Sound of someone entering the lower door. SUSAN *and* ROSS *move to the kitchen, where they look at the TV secu-rity screen.*

SUSAN: . . . that's just Mrs. Ramone. . . . Alright. Now lis-ten: there is *some* record of . . . *(She takes out her album of Jamaica and starts looking through it.)* . . . there is some record of this fellow's face . . . some-thing he left his *fingerprints* on . . .

Sound of a key being turned in a lock. ROSS *looks, fright-ened, up at the security screen, to show the old woman,* MRS. RAMONE, *letting herself into the apartment across the way.*

Hold on the screen.

SUSAN: *(VO)* . . . and when you find that, the police can identify . . .

ANGLE, CU ROSS.

ROSS: The security camera. *(Pause)*

ANGLE. ROSS AND SUSAN.

There was a security camera at the hotel. They said they kept the tapes. For insurance . . .

80. EXT. STREET CORNER. DAY.

A clean, new car pulls up, around the corner from the small Japanese bodega, which is now festooned with Irish decorations. SUSAN *is in the driver's seat.* ROSS *emerges from a doorway and climbs into the car.*

ANGLE. INT. THE CAR.

DISSOLVE TO:

81. EXT. THRUWAY. DAY.
The car on the thruway.

82. ANGLE. INT.
SUSAN *driving,* ROSS *sitting beside her.*
ROSS: . . . I have very little money.
She nods, reaches in her purse, and hands him a wallet. He takes the money.
ROSS: I don't have a passport.
SUSAN: . . . you don't need a passport for Jamaica.
Pause.

83. EXT. LAGUARDIA AIRPORT. DAY.
Their car, pulling past the International Departures sign.

84. ANGLE. INT. THE CAR. DAY. ROSS AND SUSAN.
ROSS: . . . when they find Lang's dead . . .
SUSAN: . . . you'll be in Jamaica.
ROSS: . . . left my bloody fingerprints all over the apartment.
SUSAN *nods.*
ROSS: And I'm the only one with a motive to've wanted him dead.
SUSAN: *(Nods)* Well, let's clear it up, then.
Pause.
ROSS: Don't you doubt me for an instant . . . ?
SUSAN: I don't doubt you for an instant, no.
ROSS: Why . . . ?
SUSAN: . . . because I'm *stuck* on . . . I believe we have a problem.

ROSS: . . . and when they find out Lang's been killed . . .
SUSAN: . . . you'll be in Jamaica . . . *(She looks out the windshield.)* I think they've already found out.
ROSS *looks out the windshield as the car stops.*

85. ANGLE, ROSS'S POV.
Two STATE TROOPERS *coming down the line of cars. A roadblock. They interrogate the people in the second car ahead.*

ANGLE. INT. THE CAR.
SUSAN *and* ROSS *look at each other.* ROSS *moves to open the passenger door, to get out.* SUSAN *restrains him. She gestures toward her side mirror.*

ANGLE, SUSAN'S POV.
In the side mirror, we see another pair of TROOPERS, *working up the line of cars.*

ANGLE.
ROSS *looks out his mirror and sees the same.*

ANGLE. IN THE CAR.
The TROOPERS *are at the car ahead. We hear their interrogation.*
TROOPER: *(VO)* See your driver's license, please . . . ?
MAN IN CAR: *(VO)* . . . what's the . . .
TROOPER: *(VO)* Please, may I see your Driver's License, sir . . . please keep your hands where I can see them.
ANGLE.
ROSS, *looking out the windshield.*

ANGLE, ROSS'S POV.
The TROOPER *at the car ahead, studying a photograph, and comparing it with the* DRIVER *of the car ahead.*

ANGLE. ROSS AND SUSAN.

TROOPER: *(VO)* . . . thank you, sir. Please drive on . . .

ROSS *and* SUSAN *look at each other.* ROSS *shrugs "good-bye . . ." The* TROOPER *starts to knock on the window. He wears a green carnation boutonniere.*

TROOPER: Good morning, ma'am, sir, would you please . . .

ROSS: *(Sotto. To* SUSAN*)* Scream at me. *(Pause)* Scream at me . . .

SUSAN: *(To* ROSS*)* Well, this is the end. This is the end, you stupid *Mick.* D'you think I wanted to go? You think I wanted to go to your Drunken Family. You call it a Holiday, it's a *disgrace*—it's eight in the morning, and you're *drunk,* And You Forgot the Tickets, and you expect me to drive Home, and . . .

ROSS *turns his face away in shame* . . .

TROOPER: Ma'am, would you pull the car over, please, and . . .

SUSAN: I'm *not* pulling the car over. I'm *not* going to Toronto, and I'm *not* going Anywhere But Home, and dump this *disgrace* . . . *(To* ROSS*)* Do you hear me? You think it's *charming?* You think it's all Irish and Charming to behave this way? You're a *disgrace* . . . you *disgust* me . . . you . . .

ANGLE. EXT. THE CAR.

TROOPER: *(Waving them on)* . . . alright, move on . . . keep moving out of the terminal please . . .

SUSAN: *(As she drives away)* You *bet* I'm going to keep moving out of the term——*(To* ROSS*)* Don't you smile at me . . .

ANGLE.

The Air Jamaica sign as the car pulls past it and away, out of the terminal.

86. INT. THE CAR. DAY.
The car on the expressway.
ROSS: . . . how do I get to Jamaica . . . ?
SUSAN: The traditional way. You fly.
ROSS: . . . they're looking for me at the airports . . .
SUSAN *looks up and wrenches the car across several lanes to make an exit.*
SUSAN: . . . they aren't looking for you in Boston.
ROSS: How do you know?
SUSAN: St. Paddy's Day in Boston? They aren't gonna be looking too hard for much of anything.

ANGLE.
The road sign their car is just passing under. It reads, "New England Thruway. North. Providence. Boston."

DISSOLVE TO:

87. EXT. HIGHWAY OASIS/REST STOP. DAY.
SUSAN *coming out of the convenience store with a cardboard coffee tray. Camera takes her to the car, where* ROSS *is sitting, looking at a small piece of paper. Camera takes her into the car. She puts the coffee tray on the windshield.*

88. ANGLE. INT. THE CAR AS IT DRIVES OFF.
SUSAN *reaches over, takes the piece of paper, and looks at it.*

ANGLE, INS.
It is a book of matches from the Barclay House, Jamaica.

ANGLE.
SUSAN, *as she hands the matchbook to* ROSS. *From a small paper bag she takes a roll of film. As she speaks, she takes*

her camera, in its distinctive red case, from her purse,
loads the film into it.
ROSS: . . . they played me for such a fool.
Pause.
   SUSAN *considers, then speaks.*
SUSAN: Y'know . . .
Pause.
ROSS: . . . what?
SUSAN: You just had some bad training. Early on.
ROSS: I don't understand.
SUSAN: *(Nods)* You advertise yourself as someone with a
     Low Self-Opinion . . . *(Shrugs)* You're going to Draw
     Flies.
ROSS: . . . what if I'm guilty?
SUSAN: I'm a big girl.
Pause.
   She takes a pair of sunglasses out of the coffee tray and
hands them to ROSS.
SUSAN: . . . here . . . conceal yourself.
ROSS: *(About to put them on)* Won't that look
     suspicious . . . ?
SUSAN: Not on a man going to Jamaica . . .
He looks at her admiringly.
ROSS: . . . you take *everything* in stride . . . ?
SUSAN: . . . next time be born Italian.
She puts the loaded camera on the dashboard.

DISSOLVE TO:

89. EXT. LOGAN AIRPORT. DAY.
A blinking sign reading, "Happy St. Patrick's Day." The
highway approach. The terminal instruction signs. One
reads, "Air Jamaica."

90. ANGLE.
ROSS *and* SUSAN, *as their car pulls into the terminal.*
ROSS: I don't have a ticket.
SUSAN *nods, "I've thought of that, too." She gestures
down at the seat.* ROSS *looks down.*

ANGLE, ROSS'S POV.
*In her bag is the Jamaica album. She extracts the album
and turns to the page that holds the unused ticket. We see*
ROSS's *hand take the ticket.*

ANGLE.
The two of them in the car.
ROSS: You've thought of everything.
SUSAN: It ain't hard to do. I'm fond of you.
*He looks at her. The car slows and stops for traffic. He
reaches over, and, impulsively, kisses her. They kiss for a
while.*
SUSAN: *(As she draws back)* . . . crikey . . .
We hear car horns honking. SUSAN *puts the car in gear and
drives on.*

91. INT. AIRLINE TERMINAL. DAY.
We see, out the window, SUSAN *and* ROSS. *She double-
parks her car, and they start to get out of it. We see her
reach onto the dashboard and pick up the camera.*

ANGLE.
The car. They walk away from it, SUSAN *clutching the
camera. Camera takes them across the street, to a* VENDOR
selling shamrocks.
SUSAN: . . . the ticket . . . !
She runs back to the car.

ANGLE. FROM INSIDE THE TERMINAL.
ROSS, *looking around, worried.* SUSAN *comes back and joins him, takes his arm, and hesitates. Buys them both green carnations.*

92. INT. AIRLINE TERMINAL. DAY.
SUSAN *and* ROSS *enter. He is frightened and begins to look furtively around.*

   SUSAN, *to cover her nervousness, draws him to her and puts the green carnation into his lapel.*
SUSAN: *(Sotto)* . . . when in Rome . . .
Beat.

   They look at each other. SUSAN *draws* ROSS *to her and kisses him.*
SUSAN: Get the tape. Come back safe. Let's clear the thing
     up . . .
He kisses her again.
SUSAN: . . . I know . . .
They are jostled apart by several JAPANESE PASSENGERS *being directed by an* AIRLINE EMPLOYEE.
ROSS: I . . .
SUSAN: *I* know you're innocent. Now, you go prove it and
     come back to me.
AIRLINE EMPLOYEE: . . . if you have your ticket, you can
     proceed directly to the gate.

ANGLE.
SUSAN *and* ROSS, *moving to the gate.*
ROSS: . . . what will you do?
SUSAN: I'll worry about you.
They move to the security check-in area. There is a very long line.
ROSS: *(Looking around)* . . . I'm going to be here an
     hour . . .

SUSAN: You'll be safe. They won't be looking for you up
    here.
He takes his place in line behind a MOTHER *with an unruly*
THREE-YEAR-OLD CHILD. *She is eating an ice cream.*
CHILD: . . . I want my book.
MOTHER: I'll give you your book when you've finished
    your ice cream . . .
SUSAN: . . . take my camera . . . take the camera, get a pic-
    ture of the girl who was the "Princess . . ."
ROSS: Can that help?
SUSAN: It can't hurt. If you think of any other *thing* . . .
    something he *touched,* or . . . you have your
    ticket . . . ?
He pats a pocket.
ROSS: . . . how can I thank you?
*She gestures, with a finger to her lips, meaning, "That's
not necessary between you and me."*
    Beat.
    She nods, hesitates a moment, and moves off. ROSS
moves to the back of the security line. He moves past two
OLDER PEOPLE, *one holding a newspaper.*
FIRST OLD PERSON: . . . did you see in the Paper this morn-
    ing . . . ?
SECOND OLD PERSON: Well, you see, that's why I won't go
    to New York . . . in the *older* days . . .
ROSS *looks around.*

ANGLE, ROSS'S POV.
A MASS. STATE TROOPER, *by a ticket booth some distance
away.*

ANGLE.
ROSS, *as he turns back to the line and puts on his dark
glasses. The* OLD COUPLE *recedes into the distance.*

FIRST OLD PERSON: . . . but it *is* becoming more dangerous. It's not just *statistics* . . . there's a basic *change,*
in . . .

ANGLE.

ROSS, *in the back of the security line. The* MOTHER *is still
dealing with the unruly* CHILD. *The* CHILD *takes the book
from the* MOTHER *and drops it on the floor.*

MOTHER: I *told* you that you could not have the book until
you've finished with . . .

ROSS *stoops and hands the book back.*

MOTHER: . . . thank you. Now: Fine: Now you've *torn* it,
you've *torn* your book, and you've gotten your . . .

The CHILD *flings the book again, and* ROSS *retrieves it. An*
AIR JAMAICA EMPLOYEE *comes up to the group.*

AIR JAMAICA EMPLOYEE: . . . you can move to the head of
the line, if you like . . .

The MOTHER *begins gathering up the* CHILD, *her packages, the* CHILD's *teddy bear. She addresses* ROSS.

MOTHER: . . . could you help us, please . . . ?

ROSS *picks up the stroller, and they all move to the head of
the line. They prepare to go through the security screen.*

MOTHER: *(To the* CHILD*)* You've torn your book, and I'm
not getting you another one.

SECURITY EMPLOYEE: *(To the* CHILD*)* We'll have to put
Teddy through the machine. *(To the* MOTHER*)* Ma'am.

MOTHER: Yes. One moment . . . *(To* CHILD*)* Now, I *need*
you to do what I *tell* you to do . . .

She hands the bear to the SECURITY PERSON, *who puts it
on the conveyor.*

SECURITY EMPLOYEE: *(To* ROSS*)* . . . and, ʝir, you'll need to
put through your camera. *(Pause)* Your camera, sir. I
promise you it won't hurt the film.

ROSS: *(Taking off the camera)* Yes. Of course.

CHILD: I don't want my Bear to go in the Machine . . .

SECURITY EMPLOYEE: . . . I *promise* you . . . look: Look,
would you like to come back and see . . .

MOTHER: No. Thank you, I don't think . . . *(To the* CHILD*)*
Oh, now *look*—you've gotten your filthy fingerprints
All over the Book. You've *Torn* it, and . . .

ROSS: *(To himself)* . . . the Book!

MOTHER: You've got your *fingerprints* . . .

ROSS: *(To himself)* He left his fingerprints in the tennis
book . . .

ROSS *steps out of the line and starts toward the exit—
toward* SUSAN.

AIRLINE EMPLOYEE: *(Stopping* ROSS, *by way of being help-
ful)* . . . if you have your ticket, you don't need to
return to the . . .

ROSS: *(As he takes out his ticket)* Yes. I *have* my ticket . . .
Thank you . . .

ANGLE, INS.
The ticket in ROSS*'s hand as he holds it up.*
ROSS: *(VO)* . . . if you'd *excuse* me . . .
AIRLINE EMPLOYEE: *(VO)* I just . . .

ANGLE.
At the security scanner. The CHILD *is screaming, and the*
SECURITY EMPLOYEE *is saying:* "Look, see, come around
here, you can see, nothing is happening to your bear . . ."
The MOTHER *takes the* CHILD *around the back. Our angle
shows the teddy bear going through and* ROSS, *in the BG,
hurrying away.*

ANGLE.
*At the security scanner. We see the teddy bear start to go
through and the camera come up on the screen. We see*

ROSS *and the* EMPLOYEE *in the* BG. *We see the camera case
start into the scanner picture. It holds a strange object.
The* SECURITY EMPLOYEE *stoops to return the teddy bear
to the* CHILD *and so takes her attention from the screen.*

ANGLE.
Tight on ROSS *and the* AIRLINE EMPLOYEE.
ROSS: . . . yes, please, *thank* you.
*He replaces the ticket in his lapel pocket. As he turns the
ticket moves into a tight INS. and we see it is made out for
the destination "Caracas, Venezuela."*

ANGLE.
*The scanner. We see the strange object the camera case
holds is a gun. In the BG we see* ROSS, *hurrying out of the
airport as the* SECURITY EMPLOYEE *hands back the* CHILD
to the MOTHER *and begins to return to the screen.*

93. EXT. THE AIRPORT. DAY.
As ROSS *comes out, running after* SUSAN.

EXT. THE AIRPORT. DEPARTURE AREA. DAY.
ROSS, *exiting the building. A group of* JAPANESE TOURISTS
getting on a Transit Authority bus.

ANGLE, ROSS'S POV.
SUSAN, *a few feet from her car, walking toward the car.*

ANGLE.
ROSS, *as he calls to her,* "Susan. Susan," *and removes his
dark glasses. Camera tilts down from CU to INS, showing
"Caracas, Venezuela," on the ticket.*

ANGLE.

SUSAN, *as she turns to* ROSS, *questioningly. She then looks behind her, at a Town Car double-parked behind her car, at which we see* MCCUNE. MCCUNE *mimes, "What's happening?"*

ANGLE.

SUSAN *mimes back, "I don't know . . ." She turns back toward* ROSS.

ANGLE.

ROSS, *as he starts to speak. The security alarms go off inside the airport.* ROSS *turns, then turns back.*

ANGLE, ROSS'S POV.

SUSAN, *and the car behind her. The car is being ticketed by a* POLICEMAN. *The* POLICEMAN *looks up at the alarm and goes on writing the ticket.* SUSAN *looks at* ROSS. ROSS *looks at the* POLICEMAN *and steers* SUSAN *onto the Transit Authority bus.*

94. INT. THE BUS. DAY.

SUSAN *and* ROSS *in the stairwell.*

SUSAN: *(Sotto)* . . . what happened . . .

Camera tracks with them as they move through the bus, past several JAPANESE TOURISTS, *to the back.*

ROSS: . . . the *book*—the tennis book! The torn tennis
     book—it's got his fingerprints in it.

SUSAN: . . . who . . . ?

ROSS: Dell!

SUSAN: . . . what *happened* back there . . . ?

ROSS: I don't know.

ANGLE.
On SUSAN, *as she looks out the back window of the bus.*

ANGLE, ROSS'S POV.
The Town Car with MCCUNE *and* DELL *behind them.* DELL
gestures, "What are you going to do . . . ?"

ANGLE.
On SUSAN, *as she gestures, "Stick with me."*
ROSS: . . . we've got to get that book.

ANGLE. SUSAN AND ROSS.
SUSAN: . . . where is it?
ROSS: In my desk at home. We've got to get back to New
    York.
The bus is stopped in traffic.
SUSAN: *(Nods)* Well, I think the airport's closed to us.
    Alright. We'll get into *town* . . .
BUS DRIVER, *on a PA.*
BUS DRIVER: . . . friends, been a bit of a drunken revelry
    up ahead, accident in the tunnel, somebody had a lit-
    tle too much St. Pat's Day, I'm afraid we're going
    to . . .

ANGLE. ROSS, AS HE LOOKS OUT OF THE BUS.

ANGLE, ROSS'S POV.
A sign reads, "Take the Water Shuttle to Boston."
BUS DRIVER: *(VO)* . . . be stuck here for some little while.

95. INT. ON THE WATER SHUTTLE. DAY.
*The Transit bus and the airport traffic jam in the BG. Two
Japanese tourists, a* MAN *and his* DAUGHTER, *a young*

woman carrying a tube marked "Souvenir of the Boston Aquarium," getting onto the shuttle, followed by SUSAN *and* ROSS. *The tourists converse in Japanese, move past the camera, as does a* MAN IN A PEACOAT.

ANGLE. ON THE BOAT.
ROSS *and* SUSAN *move to the bow.*
SUSAN: . . . how did they get on to you?
ROSS: . . . I don't know . . .
SUSAN: No matter . . . no matter at all.
We hear the boat blowing its whistle, and, in the stern, see the DECKHAND *about to draw in the gangplank. We see* MCCUNE *getting out of the Town Car and starting toward the water shuttle. She is almost to the gangplank when we hear a car horn honking and see* MCCUNE *speaking to someone in the backseat. We hear the boat's whistle blow again and see* MCCUNE, *alerted, start back toward the water shuttle. But as she arrives we see the gangplank is drawn up, and the boat is starting off into the water as* MCCUNE *argues heatedly with an official on the pier.*

96. EXT. WATER SHUTTLE. DAY.
SUSAN *and* ROSS *standing by a huge sign reading, "Passengers are barred by law from interrupting or communicating with the operating crew." The sign is attached to a wire grating, through which we see the ladder going up to the boat's bridge.*
SUSAN: No matter at all.
The tourists come up to the bow and continue conversing in Japanese as the FATHER *admonishes the* YOUNG WOMAN.
SUSAN: No. Matter. We'll . . . alright. We'll call New
        York . . . we'll get someone to get your book . . .

ROSS: . . . who can we call?

SUSAN: We'll call Mr. Klein, we'll call the Boss . . . I bet
    you there's a phone on the boat. Don't worry. Good.
    The tennis book!

*She kisses him and starts to the back of the boat, into the
enclosed cabin area.*

ANGLE.

On ROSS. *He stands alone as the* TICKET TAKER *comes
down the deck, taking tickets. He takes the tickets from
the* JAPANESE FATHER *and* DAUGHTER, *and the third passenger, a* MAN *seated looking out at the water. He
approaches* ROSS.

TICKET TAKER: Ticket, please . . .

ROSS *reaches for his ticket, distractedly, and hands it to
the man. The* TICKET TAKER *continues down the deck and
turns back to* ROSS.

TICKET TAKER: . . . sir . . . ?

ROSS *walks over to him.*

ANGLE.

On ROSS *and the* TICKET TAKER.

TICKET TAKER: *(Laughing)* I'm afraid this boat don't go
    that far.

ROSS: . . . what?

TICKET TAKER: . . . you got a ticket here for Venezuela.

He laughs and hands the ticket back to ROSS, *who digs in
his pocket.*

TICKET TAKER: *(Making conversation)* . . . why would you
    want to go *there* . . . ?

ROSS: . . . what?

TICKET TAKER: . . . why would you want to go *there* . . . ?

Pause.

ROSS: *(As it occurs to him)* . . . because they have no extradition treaty.

The TICKET TAKER *shrugs, takes some money from* ROSS, *and moves off, through the barred gate and up to the bridge.*

DELL: *(VO)* . . . and so we come to the End of a Perfect Day.

ANGLE.

On ROSS *as he turns and sees* DELL, *who has come up next to him, dressed in a peacoat and watch cap. We see* DELL *look beyond* ROSS *and see* SUSAN *come into the shot.* DELL *looks at* SUSAN *as if to say, "And now."*

SUSAN: Clang, clang, end-of-the-line.

ROSS: How does it end?

SUSAN: You kidnapped me. You killed, you did it all for money, and now, trapped, overcome with remorse, you took your own life. What could be more appropriate?

ROSS: And if I don't cooperate?

SUSAN: Well, I'm afraid you have no choice.

Pause.

ROSS: Why?

SUSAN: Why? Cause Money Makes the Mare Go.

He looks at her.

SUSAN: Nobody lives forever. The important thing is to *enjoy* yourself. *(Pause. To* DELL*)* Kill him.

ROSS *moves away past the grating leading up to the bridge. He tries to shake it and finds it unmovable. He moves to the rear of the boat, where we see the Japanese* FATHER *and the* DAUGHTER *holding the "Souvenir of the Boston Aquarium" tube. The* JAPANESE MAN *bows toward* ROSS *as he moves past, then separates himself from his*

DAUGHTER, *moves to the stern, and begins taking photographs.*

ANGLE.
On ROSS, *as he moves away from* DELL.

ANGLE, ROSS'S POV.
At the waist of the boat, DELL *and* SUSAN *talking.* DELL *nods, cycles the pistol, and advances slowly toward* ROSS.

ANGLE.
ROSS, *looking about for an avenue of escape.*

ANGLE.
ROSS, *the* JAPANESE MAN *next to him.* DELL *advancing in the BG.*
JAPANESE MAN: *(VO. Speaking suddenly in English)* . . . didn't your mother have a dog named Paddy?

ANGLE.
ROSS *and the* JAPANESE MAN. ROSS *looks at him incredulously.*
JAPANESE MAN: . . . didn't she have a dog named Paddy?
    (Gestures at the green carnation in ROSS's *lapel.)*
    Well, then, this must be a big day for you . . . see if
    you can get him to tell you where the *Process* is.
    *(Pause. He gestures down to a small radio mike,
    stuck to the rail.)* You're doing fine. *(He bows slightly
    and retreats, calling to his daughter in Japanese.)*

ANGLE.
DELL, *approaching* ROSS. *The two alone on the fantail.*
DELL *looks over his shoulder at the approaching Boston skyline.*

DELL: . . . 'fraid we don't have too much time . . .
He gestures with the pistol, chambers a round.
ROSS: . . . they'll find bullet holes in me.
DELL: You shot yourself, and then jumped overboard.
Sound of the boat's whistle, as it approaches the dock.
DELL: 'S been a slice.
ROSS: What did you do with the Process . . . ?
DELL: Is that your last request . . . ?
ROSS *nods.* DELL *shrugs, "Alright, then." He starts to
speak, as if to say, "The answer is obvious . . ."*
DELL: We took the Report, and . . .
He is drowned out by the sound of the boat's whistle.
DELL *finishes speaking. He looks around to see he is unob-
served.*

ANGLE.
DELL's *hand, as it comes up with the pistol.*

ANGLE, CU.
ROSS *looks down at the pistol, then looks around for help.*

ANGLE, ROSS'S POV.
The JAPANESE MAN *is gone. The boat seems deserted
except for the* JAPANESE WOMAN *in the cabin.*

ANGLE.
ROSS *and* DELL *as the pistol comes up to* ROSS's *head. We
hear the sound of a shot, and* DELL *drops at* ROSS's *feet.*
ROSS *looks around.*

ANGLE.
The JAPANESE WOMAN *in the cabin is lowering a short,
odd-looking rifle.*

ANGLE.

ROSS *looks down at the man at his feet. The boat slows to come to the dock. The* WOMAN *and the* JAPANESE MAN *walk back to* ROSS. *They look down at the figure of* DELL.

ROSS: And now, I suppose, you'll take the Process to Japan.

JAPANESE MAN: *(As he reveals a badge)* United States Marshal Service, actually . . .

ROSS: *(Of* DELL*)* 'D you have to kill 'im . . . ?

The MARSHAL *bends down and retrieves a dart device from* DELL's *chest.*

MARSHAL: Stun gun . . . *(to the* WOMAN*)* . . . good shooting.

ROSS: *Stun* gun . . . what if you'd *missed* . . . ?

WOMAN: *(Brightly)* Then it'd be Back to the Range for Me . . . !

As the boat pulls up to the dock, we see several vans marked, "United States Marshal Service," and ARMED MEN *on the dock.*

97. EXT. WATER SHUTTLE AT DOCK. DAY.

On the boat, ROSS *and the two* JAPANESE MARSHALS *walk toward the cabin, where we see* SUSAN. *Several* ARMED MEN *board the boat, and the* JAPANESE MARSHAL *directs them to take her into custody.*

JAPANESE MARSHAL: *(To* ROSS*)* The whole thing was set up by your boss, Mr. Klein. To steal the Process. Easy to steal it, hard to get away with the crime. 'F there's only two keys to the safe, 'n' *he* didn't want to take it *(Shrugs)* then, *you* had to. And then run away . . .

SUSAN *is led past* ROSS *and the* MARSHALS, *off the boat.*

JAPANESE MARSHAL: *(To* SUSAN*)* . . . off you go, now . . .

ANGLE.

ROSS, *as he looks after* SUSAN.

ROSS: Good-bye.

SUSAN: Oh, don't make a big thing out of it.

ROSS: What will happen to them?

JAPANESE MARSHAL: . . . 'fraid they're gonna have to spend some time in their rooms.

ANGLE, MARSHAL'S POV.

SUSAN, *as she is led off the boat.*

JAPANESE MARSHAL: *(VO)* Lordy, you've been leading us a Merry Chase . . .

ANGLE.

ROSS *and the two* MARSHALS.

ROSS: *(As he tears himself away from looking at* SUSAN*)* . . . you were watching me the entire time . . . ?

WOMAN MARSHAL: Your tax dollars at work . . . ?

JAPANESE MARSHAL: *(Surveys the scene with self-satisfaction; looks at* ROSS *for the phrase that will wrap up the association. He takes the green carnation boutonniere from* ROSS*'s buttonhole and begins to put it in his own. Self-congratulating)* Nobody looks at a Japanese tourist. *(Pause)*

ANGLE. ON THE PIER.

SUSAN *is led off in manacles by two* POLICEMEN. *She looks back at* ROSS.

SUSAN: Joe: can you help me . . . ? Joe? You're the Boy Scout . . . can I be your Good Deed? Can you help me, Joe . . . ?

Pause.

ROSS: I'm afraid you're going to have to spend some time in your room.

SUSAN, *about to be put into a waiting police van, looks back at* ROSS *and smiles. She is put into the van, which drives away, leaving* ROSS *standing on the pier.*

FADE OUT.

The

WINSLOW

BOY

A SCREENPLAY

Based on the play by
Terence Rattigan

FADE IN:

1. EXT. WINSLOW HOUSE. DAY.

Open on DICKIE WINSLOW *buying a newspaper from a kiosk and joining* ARTHUR, GRACE, *and* CATHERINE *Winslow. The camera takes them up the steps of their house. It is raining lightly. They are in their churchgoing clothes. As they mount the steps,* ARTHUR *Winslow hands his prayer books to* DICKIE *and reaches for his keys; the others hand their prayer books to* DICKIE.

ARTHUR: He's a good man.

GRACE: I'm sorry, Arthur?

ARTHUR: Good man. Pharaoh's dream. Dream of the King of Egypt. Seven Fat Years, Seven Lean Years. Good sermon.

GRACE: I couldn't *hear* him . . .

They enter the front hallway.

2. INT. WINSLOW HALLWAY. DAY.

GRACE: *(Cont'd.)* What's the use in being good if you're inaudible?

DICKIE *sets down the books;* CATHERINE *et al. begin taking off their wraps;* DICKIE *goes to the gramophone.*

CATHERINE: A problem in Ethics for you, Father.

DICKIE: Not everything is a problem in ethics.

CATHERINE: Never prove it by me . . .

DICKIE: What, never?

CATHERINE: Well, hardly ever.

ARTHUR: "And the seven fat cows were devoured by the seven lean and hungry cows."

DICKIE: Yes, and don't I feel like those lean and hungry
     COWS.

ARTHUR: My point precisely.

VIOLET: *(As she bobs into the room)* Lunch in about an
     hour, sir.

GRACE: *(Looking out of the open front door)* Oh, my. It's
     going to rain. *(She closes the door.)*

ARTHUR: I could have told you that, I feel it in my leg.

A MAID *enters and starts taking coats.*

DICKIE: *(Looking into the hallway)* Excuse me, would you
     please mind the gramophone?

ARTHUR: . . . the center of a well-regulated home.

GRACE *takes* CATHERINE *aside for a whispered conference.*
CATHERINE *nods.* GRACE *passes into the dining room and
begins to direct the laying of the table.*

DICKIE: It helps me concentrate.

ARTHUR: Concentrate on what, pray?

DICKIE *and* ARTHUR *proceed into the hallway near the
entrance to the drawing room. Beyond them we see the*
WORKMAN, *putting up the Christmas tree, as* CATHERINE
climbs the front staircase.

ARTHUR: *(Cont'd.)* . . . Catherine . . . ?

CATHERINE: Yes, Father, I just wanted to see about the . . .

DICKIE: . . . to *study*, Father . . . to study . . .

ARTHUR: . . . what did you say?

DICKIE: I said, the gramophone, the music of the gramo-
     phone helps me to study, Father.

ARTHUR: *Study* is not what you appeared to be involved in
     when I came downstairs last night, your friend and
     you.

DICKIE: Edwina, Father, Edwina had just stopped by to,
     she'd just stopped by on the way from Graham's
     dance to fetch a book, and . . .

ARTHUR: And so, you are involved with her in what, a sort of what, a "reading club"?

2A. INT. WINSLOW HOUSE, CATHERINE'S ROOM/UPSTAIRS LANDING. DAY.
A suffragette poster, many books. CATHERINE *darts in, checks her hair in the mirror, reaches in her desk.*

ANGLE. INSIDE THE DESK.
She takes from the desk a book and puts it under her arm. From behind the book she takes a packet of cigarettes and puts it in her reticule. She reaches for matches, shakes the box, finds it empty, and puts it back.

ANGLE. ON CATHERINE AT THE DESK.
She starts out of the room, goes back, opens the drawer of her desk, and takes out a ring box. She opens it.

ANGLE, INS. THE RING BOX CONTAINS A DIAMOND ENGAGE-MENT RING.

ANGLE. ON CATHERINE.
She closes the box and puts it in her pocket.

3. INT. WINSLOW DRAWING ROOM. DAY.
Beyond we see the WORKMAN *putting up the tree and* GRACE *coming into the drawing room. She casts a glance up the stairs.*
DICKIE: *(VO)* A right to be a certain measure, a certain measure, Father, of, for want of a better word, of autonomy.
GRACE *enters the drawing room.*
GRACE: I'm sorry, what were we discussing?

DICKIE: Edwina.

GRACE: Edwina, what a fast and flighty . . . *(She looks at* DICKIE *and sees his hurt expression.)* I'm sorry, Dickie, you're rather keen on her, *aren't* you . . . ?

ARTHUR: You would have had ample evidence of that fact, had you discovered them in the attitude in which I came on them last night.

DICKIE: We were doing the Bunny Hug.

GRACE: . . . the what, dear?

DICKIE: The Bunny Hug.

CATHERINE *enters.*

CATHERINE: It's like the Turkey Trot. Only more dignified.

4. INT. WINSLOW DRAWING ROOM. DAY.
They enter the drawing room. Beyond them we see the garden and the terrace.

DICKIE: No, more like the Fox-Trot, really, Fox-Trot, or the Kangaroo Glide.

ANGLE, INS. ON THE DESKTOP, IN THE DRAWING ROOM.
An old magnifying glass, next to it a box of matches.
CATHERINE*'s hand takes the matches.*

ARTHUR: More to the point, whichever animal was responsible for the posture which I found you and your friend in last night . . .

GRACE *clears her throat.*

ARTHUR: *(Cont'd.)* Or let me say, to make an end, that I doubt, I *doubt* the gramophone aids you in what you call your studies.

GRACE: *(At the window)* Yes. It's raining.

She casts a glance at CATHERINE, *who looks out at the rain and down at a small watch pinned to her shirtwaist, then shrugs at her mother.*

DICKIE: Ah ha . . . ah ha . . .

ARTHUR *still feeling in his pocket.*

ARTHUR: . . . has anybody got a *coin*? *(He inclines his head toward the workman setting up the tree.)*

DICKIE: . . . and at this Festive *Season*, Father, at this Festive *Season*—to throw it to me, to bring that up again . . .

GRACE: Nobody's bringing that up . . .

VIOLET *comes in, takes a drinks tray and newspapers from a* MAID, *and brings it forward. The* MAID *leaves.*

DICKIE: Yes, they are. Ronnie. Ronnie. Ronnie Got Into Osbourne, as I did Not. Why? As he *Applies* himself . . . and Ronnie . . .

ARTHUR *looks at* DICKIE, *indicating the presence of* VIOLET, *and* DICKIE *subsides.*

VIOLET: Good sermon, Miss?

CATHERINE: *(Looking out the window)* Mmm? *"Joseph interprets Pharaoh's dreams."*

VIOLET: Oh, Lord, it's coming down . . .

CATHERINE *walks to the bookcase and takes down a book, looks out the window, and sits.* VIOLET *leaves.*

ARTHUR: Anybody got a *coin* . . . ?

DICKIE: If I may, sir, I'm, going to my room.

ARTHUR: *(Of the gramophone)* Might I suggest you take that object with you?

DICKIE: May I ask why?

ARTHUR: It's out of place in a drawing room.

He walks DICKIE *to the door of the drawing room.* DICKIE *leaves, and* ARTHUR, GRACE, *and* CATHERINE *move through to the study.*

5. INT. WINSLOW STUDY/DRAWING ROOM. DAY.

ARTHUR: *(Cont'd.)* It's pelting down out there.

GRACE: What, dear?

ARTHUR: I said it's raining.

He sits down next to his Bible with his drink and lights a cigarette. In the background a MAID *lights the drawing room fire.*

ARTHUR: *(Cont'd. Of his drink as he sits by the fire in the fireplace)* . . . quite insufficient for the Lean and Hungry cows. *(He takes a pair of spectacles from his vest pocket and holds them up to examine* CATHERINE's *book.)* What are you reading?

CATHERINE: Len Rogers's memoirs.

ARTHUR *puts his spectacles down on the desk, next to the large magnifying glass.*

GRACE: And who is Len Rogers, dear?

CATHERINE: He was a Trades Union Leader.

GRACE: Was he a Radical?

CATHERINE: I'd say so.

GRACE: Does John know your . . . Political . . . ?

CATHERINE: Oh, yes.

GRACE: And he still wants to marry you?

CATHERINE: Seems to.

CATHERINE *nods to her mother.*

   Pause.

GRACE: Oh, by the way, I've asked John to come early for lunch.

ARTHUR: *(Who has been almost dozing off)* What?

CATHERINE: He's coming early for lunch.

ARTHUR: Mm.

CATHERINE: You won't let me down and Forbid the Match, or anything, will you, because I warn you, If you do, I shall elope.

ARTHUR: *(Taking her hand)* Never fear, my dear. I'm far too delighted at the prospect of getting you off our hands at last. Does *Desmond* know, by the way . . . ?

CATHERINE: I'm not sure I like that "at last."

ARTHUR: Have you told Desmond, yet?

GRACE: Do you love him, dear?

CATHERINE: John? Yes, I do.

GRACE: Do you? You don't behave as if you were in love.

CATHERINE: How does one behave as if one is in love?

ARTHUR: One doesn't read . . .

He pats his pockets for his spectacles. CATHERINE *finds them on the desk and hands them to him.*

ARTHUR: *(Cont'd. Reading the book)* One doesn't read *The Social Evil and the Social Good.* One Reads Lord Byron . . .

ANGLE, INS.

ARTHUR *puts his spectacles and the book down on the desk. We read the cover of the book,* "The Social Evil and the Social Good, *by Len Rogers."*

CATHERINE: Ah, yes, is that so?

ANGLE. ON THE ROOM.

CATHERINE: *(Cont'd.)* I see . . .

GRACE: *(Sighing)* I don't think you modern girls have the feelings our generation did.

CATHERINE: Very well, Mother. I love John in every way that a woman can love a man. Does that satisfy you?

GRACE *rises and moves, embarrassed, to the window.*

GRACE: . . . just look at the rain.

There is the sound of a doorbell. And the family begins to arrange itself.

GRACE: *(Cont'd. Turning from the window)* Hullo, I thought there was someone in the Garden.

CATHERINE: Where?

GRACE: *(Pointing)* Over there, do you see?

CATHERINE: *(Leaving the window)* Well, whoever it is, is getting terribly wet.

There is the sound of voices outside in the hall.

GRACE: Was that John?

CATHERINE: It sounded like it.

GRACE: *(After listening)* Yes, it's John. *(To* CATHERINE*)* Quick! In the drawing room!

CATHERINE: All right.

She dashes across toward the drawing room.

GRACE: Here! You've forgotten your bag.

She darts to the table and picks it up.

ARTHUR: *(Startled)* What on earth is going on?

GRACE: *(Whispers)* We're leaving you alone with John. When you've finished cough or something.

ARTHUR: *(Testily)* What do you mean, or something?

GRACE: I know. Knock on the floor with your stick—three times. Then we'll come in.

ARTHUR: You don't think that might look a trifle coincidental?

GRACE: Sh!

GRACE and CATHERINE *walk into the drawing room, closing the adjoining doors behind them, and stand by the hall door to eavesdrop.* ARTHUR *goes into the hallway.*

6. INT. WINSLOW HALLWAY. DAY.

VIOLET *takes* JOHN's *rain-soaked umbrella and coat by the front door. The* WORKMAN *passes through the hallway, tugging his hat, taking his toolbox with him.*

ARTHUR: 'S anybody got a *coin* . . . ?

VIOLET: *(Announcing)* Mr. Watherstone.

JOHN WATHERSTONE *approaches, a well-set-up young man in his late twenties, wearing a morning coat and striped trousers. In the dining room a* MAID *continues with preparations for lunch.*

ARTHUR: How are you, John? Got a coin . . . ?

JOHN *feels in his vest pocket.*

ARTHUR: *(Cont'd.)* Good of you to come. I'm glad to see
    you . . .

JOHN *gives* ARTHUR *a coin and looks, as if to say, "Will
this do?"*

ARTHUR: *(Cont'd.)* Yes, thanks. Violet . . .

VIOLET *comes over, and* ARTHUR *motions her to give the
coin to the departing* WORKMAN.

JOHN: How do you do, sir?

ARTHUR: Let's sit, shall we? My arthritis's troubling me a
    bit.

They move toward the study.

JOHN: I'm sorry to hear that, sir. Catherine told me it was
    better.

ARTHUR: It was better, now it's worse. Do you smoke . . . ?

7. INT. WINSLOW BACKSTAIRS HALLWAY. DAY.

VIOLET *takes a shawl down off a peg and starts out after
the* WORKMAN. *As a* MAID *passes her with a tray of food
for the dining room,* VIOLET *tastes a bit.*

VIOLET: . . . stay outta the study.

8. EXT. WINSLOW GARDEN. DAY.

ANGLE.

In the garden, the WORKMAN, *walking quickly, his head
down in the rain.* VIOLET, *hurrying up to him, gives him a
coin.*

ANGLE.

Over the shoulder, back of a BOY *in a naval uniform.
Standing in the rain, he retreats into a niche in the garden
wall to avoid being seen by* VIOLET.

    In the BG we see the WORKMAN *pass through the garden
gate and the gate slam and swing open again.*

9. INT. WINSLOW STUDY. DAY.

ARTHUR *and* JOHN, *getting settled; beyond them the window, and the garden in the rain.* ARTHUR *offers his cigarette case to* JOHN.

 Pause while JOHN *lights his cigarette and* ARTHUR *watches him.*

ARTHUR: Well, now I understand you wish to marry my daughter.

JOHN: Yes, sir. That's to say, I've proposed to her and she's done me the honor of accepting me.

ARTHUR: I see. I trust when you corrected yourself, your second statement wasn't a denial of your first?

JOHN *looks puzzled.*

ARTHUR: *(Cont'd.)* I mean, of course, you do *really* wish to marry her?

JOHN: Of course, sir.

ARTHUR: Why, of course? There are plenty of people about who don't wish to marry her.

JOHN: I mean of course because I proposed to her.

ARTHUR: That, too, doesn't necessarily follow. However, we don't need to quibble. We'll take the sentimental side of the project for granted. As regards the more practical aspect, perhaps you won't mind if I ask you a few rather personal questions?

JOHN: Naturally not, sir. It's your duty.

ARTHUR: Quite so. Now, your income. Are you able to live on it?

JOHN: No, sir. I'm in the regular army.

ARTHUR: Yes, of course.

JOHN: But my army pay is supplemented by an allowance from my father.

ARTHUR: So I understand. Now your father's would be, I take it, about twenty-four pounds a month.

JOHN: Yes, sir, that's exactly right.

ARTHUR: So that your total income with your subaltern's pay and allowances, plus the allowance from your father, would be, I take it, about four hundred and twenty pounds a year?

JOHN: Again, exactly the figure.

ARTHUR: Well, well. It all seems perfectly satisfactory. I really don't think I need delay my congratulations any longer. I propose to settle on my daughter one-sixth of my total capital, which, worked out to the final fraction, is exactly eight hundred and thirty-three pounds, six shillings, and eight pence. But let us deal in round figures and say eight hundred and fifty pounds.

JOHN: I call that very generous, sir.

ARTHUR: Not as generous as I would have liked, I'm afraid. However—as my wife would say—beggars can't be choosers.

JOHN: Exactly, sir.

ARTHUR: Well, then, if you're agreeable to that arrangement, I don't think there's anything more we need discuss.

JOHN: No, sir.

ARTHUR: Splendid.

ARTHUR *takes his stick and raps it, with an air of studied unconcern, three times on the floor. Nothing happens.*

JOHN: Pretty rotten weather, isn't it?

ARTHUR: Yes, vile.

He raps again. Again nothing happens.

ARTHUR: *(Cont'd.)* Would you care for another cigarette?

JOHN: No, thank you, sir. I'm still smoking.

ARTHUR *takes up his stick to rap again, then thinks better of it. He goes slowly but firmly to the dining room door, which he throws open.* CATHERINE *and* GRACE *enter.*

10. EXT. WINSLOW GARDEN. DAY.
*The boy in the naval uniform (*RONNIE, *aged twelve, moving up to look in the window), i.e.,* RONNIE, *from the rear. Beyond him* JOHN *and* ARTHUR.

ANGLE, CU RONNIE, THE RAIN COMING DOWN HIS FACE.

ANGLE, RONNIE'S POV. INT. THE STUDY.

ANGLE. EXT. THE TERRACE. DAY.
RONNIE, *standing in the rain, looking in the window. He moves into some shelter and takes an envelope out of his pocket. He holds it.*

ANGLE, INS. THE ENVELOPE, BEARS AN OFFICIAL-LOOKING SEAL.

ANGLE, CU.
RONNIE, *looking down at the envelope and through the glass at his father.*

ANGLE, XCU INS. THE ENVELOPE, BEARS THE SEAL "THE ROYAL NAVAL ACADEMY, OSBOURNE."

ANGLE. INT. THE STUDY.

ANGLE.
RONNIE *looks up.*

11. INT. WINSLOW STUDY/DRAWING ROOM. DAY.
Pause.
   GRACE *is unable to repress herself. As she and* CATHERINE *talk, they move into the drawing room.*
GRACE: *(Coyly)* Well?

ARTHUR: Well, what?

GRACE: How did your little talk go?

ARTHUR: *(Testily)* I understood you weren't supposed to know we were having a little talk.

GRACE: Oh, you are infuriating! Is everything all right, John?

JOHN *nods, smiling.*

GRACE: *(Cont'd.)* Oh, I'm so glad. I really am.

JOHN: Thank you, Mrs. Winslow.

GRACE: May I kiss you? After all, I'm practically your mother, now.

JOHN: Yes. Of course.

He allows himself to be kissed.

ARTHUR: While I, by the same token, am practically your father, but if you will forgive me—

ANGLE. ON VIOLET.

She enters to clear up the drinks tray. ARTHUR *sees something in the garden.*

ARTHUR: *(Cont'd.)* Oh, now, he's gone and left the garden gate open.

ANGLE, ARTHUR'S POV.

The garden gate, swinging wildly in the rainy wind.

ANGLE.

VIOLET *gestures to the* MAID, *as if to send her out to close the gate.*

ANGLE.

On the drawing room floor, the happy foursome.

ARTHUR: *(Cont'd.)* Grace, I think we might allow ourselves a little modest celebration at luncheon. Will you find me the key of the cellars?

He goes out through the hall door.

GRACE: Yes, dear. *(She turns at the door. Coyly)* I don't
  suppose you two will mind being left alone for a few
  minutes, will you?

She follows her husband out. JOHN *goes to* CATHERINE
and kisses her.

12. EXT. WINSLOW GARDEN. DAY.

ANGLE. IN A NICHE IN THE WALL.

RONNIE *reads the letter, then puts it in his pocket.*

ANGLE. IN THE GARDEN, IN THE RAIN.

The MAID, *hurrying out to close the gate, turns back, spy-
ing* RONNIE. *Camera takes her up to* RONNIE.

13. INT. WINSLOW DRAWING ROOM. DAY.

ANGLE. INT. THE DRAWING ROOM. JOHN AND CATHERINE.

CATHERINE: Was it an ordeal?

JOHN: . . . scared to death.

CATHERINE: My poor darling—

JOHN: The annoying thing was that I had a whole lot of
  neatly turned phrases ready for him, and he wouldn't
  let me use them.

CATHERINE *opens the door onto the terrace and steps out.*

14. EXT. WINSLOW TERRACE. DAY.

CATHERINE *glances behind her, into the house, takes out
her cigarettes, and lights one.* JOHN *follows her out.*

  *She gives him a kiss, takes the ring box from her pocket,
and hands it to him. He smiles, takes the ring out, and
starts to put it on her finger.*

ANGLE, CATHERINE'S POV.
The MAID *and* RONNIE, *walking across the terrace. The* MAID *turns and goes back into the house at the kitchen level, off the screen.*
JOHN: *(Cont'd. Turning)* . . . what?
CATHERINE *steps over to the edge of the terrace. Camera takes her through.*

ANGLE. EXT. ON THE TERRACE, CATHERINE AND THE BEDRAGGLED-LOOKING RONNIE.
CATHERINE: *Ronnie.* What is it?
RONNIE: Where did Father go? Is he gone?
CATHERINE: I'll go get him.
She leads RONNIE *into the drawing room.*

15. INT. WINSLOW DRAWING ROOM. DAY.
RONNIE: *(Urgently)* No, don't. Please, Kate, don't!
CATHERINE, *halfway to the door, stops, puzzled.*
CATHERINE: What's the trouble, Ronnie?
Pause.
   RONNIE, *trembling on the edge of tears, does not answer her. She approaches him.*
CATHERINE: *(Cont'd.)* You'd better go and change.
RONNIE: No.
CATHERINE: *(Gently)* What's the trouble, darling? You can tell me.
RONNIE *looks at* JOHN.
CATHERINE: *(Cont'd.)* You know John Watherstone, Ronnie. You met him last holidays, don't you remember?
RONNIE *remains silent, obviously reluctant to talk in front of a comparative stranger.*
JOHN: *(Tactfully)* I'll disappear.
CATHERINE: *(Pointing to study)* In there, do you mind?

JOHN *goes out quietly.* CATHERINE *gently leads* RONNIE *into the hallway and settles him near the backstairs.*

16. INT. WINSLOW HALLWAY/BACKSTAIRS HALLWAY. DAY.

CATHERINE: *(Cont'd.)* Now, darling, tell me. What is it? Have you run away?

RONNIE *shakes his head, evidently not trusting himself to speak.* CATHERINE *gently removes* RONNIE's *wet cap and puts it on the newel post.*

CATHERINE: *(Cont'd.)* What is it, then?

RONNIE *pulls from his pocket the document we have seen him reading earlier and slowly hands it to her.* CATHERINE *reads it quietly.*

CATHERINE: *(Cont'd.)* Oh, God!

RONNIE: I didn't do it.

CATHERINE *rereads the letter in silence.*

RONNIE: *(Cont'd.)* Kate, I didn't. Really, I didn't.

CATHERINE: *(Abstractly)* No, darling. *(She seems uncertain what to do.)* This letter is addressed to Father. Did you open it?

RONNIE: Yes.

CATHERINE: You shouldn't have done that—

RONNIE: I was going to tear it up. Then I heard you come in from church and ran into the garden—I didn't know what to do. We could tell Father term had ended two days sooner.

CATHERINE: No, darling.

RONNIE: . . . I'm back for the Christmas Holidays, I . . .

CATHERINE: No, darling . . .

RONNIE: I didn't do it. Kate, really. I . . .

CATHERINE: You're drenched to the Skin, come on.

They encounter DICKIE, *coming downstairs.*

DICKIE: *(Cheerfully)* Hello, Ronnie, old lad. How's everything? Back early, eh?

RONNIE *turns away from him.*
CATHERINE: I'll find Mother.
DICKIE: All right.
CATHERINE *watches them go upstairs and hurries into the dining room, where the* MAID *is setting the table.* RONNIE's *wet clothes have left a puddle on the floor.*

ANGLE.
On RONNIE *walking* DICKIE *upstairs.*
DICKIE: *(Cont'd.)* What's up, then, old chap?
RONNIE: Nothing.
DICKIE: You can tell me . . .

17. INT. WINSLOW HOUSE, RONNIE'S ROOM. DAY.
An Edwardian boy's room. A poster on the wall of the Royal Naval Academy, Osbourne, an oar hanging on the wall, a rack with various naval hats.
   DICKIE *leads* RONNIE *in.*
DICKIE: *(Cont'd.)* Have you been sacked?
RONNIE *nods.*
DICKIE: *(Cont'd.)* Bad luck. What for?
RONNIE: I didn't do it.
DICKIE: No, of course you didn't.
RONNIE: Honestly. I didn't.
DICKIE: That's all right, old chap. No need to go on about
   it. I believe you.
He takes a towel from the washbasin and gently rubs down RONNIE.
DICKIE: *(Cont'd.)* I say—you're a bit damp, aren't you?
RONNIE: I've been out in the rain—
DICKIE: You're shivering a bit too, aren't you? Oughtn't
   you to go and change? I mean, we don't want you
   catching pneumonia—
RONNIE: I'm all right.

DICKIE: What is it they say you did, by the by . . . ?

GRACE *comes in, with* CATHERINE *following.* GRACE *comes quickly to* RONNIE, *who, as he sees her, turns away from* DICKIE *and runs into her arms.*

GRACE: There, darling! It's all right, now.

RONNIE *begins to cry quietly, his head buried in her dress.*

RONNIE: *(His voice muffled)* I didn't do it, Mother.

GRACE: No, darling. Of course you didn't. I know that you didn't— Now let's get out of these nasty wet clothes.

RONNIE: Don't tell Father.

GRACE: No, darling. Not yet. I promise. Come along now.

She leads him toward the door, held open by CATHERINE.

GRACE: *(Cont'd.)* Your new uniform, too. What a shame!

GRACE *motions* CATHERINE *out and closes the door.*

18. INT. WINSLOW HALLWAY/BACKSTAIRS HALLWAY. DAY.

CATHERINE *comes down the backstairs and finds* JOHN *waiting.*

JOHN: Bad news?

CATHERINE *nods.*

JOHN: *(Cont'd.)* Expelled, I suppose?

He gets his answer from her silence, while she recovers herself.

CATHERINE: God, how little imagination some people have! How can they torture a child?

JOHN: What's he supposed to have done?

She reads him the letter, hands him the letter. JOHN *takes it.*

ANGLE, INS. THE LETTER READS:

Royal Naval Academy, Osbourne
> *To Mr. Arthur Winslow, 431 Greystock Lane.*
> *I am commanded by My Lords' Commissioners*
> *of the Admiralty to inform you . . .*

CATHERINE: *(VO)* —Ten days ago. Just think what that little creature has been going through these last ten
days, entirely alone, no one to look after him, know-
ing what he had to face at the end of it!

ANGLE.
JOHN *and* CATHERINE, *as* JOHN *folds up the letter. He
passes the letter back to* CATHERINE, *and she puts it in her
pocket.*
JOHN: It does seem pretty heartless, I admit.
CATHERINE: It's cold, savage inhumanity.
JOHN: But, you must remember, darling, he's not really at
school. He's in the Service.
CATHERINE: What difference can that make?
As the MAID *passes behind them and goes into the dining
room, they move across the hallway toward the morning
room.*

19. INT. WINSLOW MORNING ROOM. DAY.
JOHN: Their ways of doing things may seem to an outsider
brutal—but at least they're always fair. There must
have been a full inquiry before they'd take a step of
this sort. What's more, if there's been a delay of ten
days, it would only have been in order to give the boy
a better chance to clear himself—
Pause.
   CATHERINE *is silent.*
JOHN: *(Cont'd.)* I'm awfully sorry. *(After a pause)* How
will your father take it?
CATHERINE: *(Simply)* It might kill him—
There is the sound of the front doorbell. VIOLET *crosses
the hallway toward the front door to greet* DESMOND.
CATHERINE: *(Cont'd.)* Oh heavens! We've got Desmond to
lunch. I'd forgotten—

CATHERINE *moves closer to* JOHN *and whispers.*

JOHN: Who?

CATHERINE: Desmond Curry—our family solicitor. Oh, Lord! *(In a hasty whisper)* Darling—be polite to him, won't you?

JOHN: Am I usually rude to your guests?

CATHERINE: No, but he doesn't know about us yet—

JOHN: Who does?

CATHERINE: *(Still in a whisper)* Yes, but he's been in love with me for years—it's a family joke—

CATHERINE *and* JOHN *enter the hallway.*

20.   INT. WINSLOW HALLWAY. DAY.

VIOLET: *(Announcing)* Mr. Curry.

DESMOND CURRY *approaches. He is a man of about forty-five.* VIOLET *exits, having put away his umbrella and coat.*

CATHERINE: Hullo, Desmond. I don't think you know John Watherstone—

DESMOND: No—but, of course, I've heard a lot about him—

JOHN: How do you do?

Pause.

DESMOND: Well, well, well. I trust I'm not early.

CATHERINE: Oh, no, dead on time, as always.

DESMOND: Capital. Good.

Pause.

   Everyone starts to speak at once.

DESMOND: *(Cont'd.)* I see you've got your *tree* . . .

JOHN: I'm sorry . . .

DESMOND: No, Catherine, please . . .

CATHERINE: It's quite all right. I was only going to ask how your shoulder was.

DESMOND: Not too well, I'm afraid. The damp, you know.

CATHERINE: I'm sorry to hear that.

DESMOND: Old cricket injury.

Another pause.

DESMOND: *(Cont'd. At length)* Well, well. It seems I'm to congratulate you both—

CATHERINE *and* JOHN *exchange a look.*

DESMOND: Violet told me, just now—at the door. Yes—I must congratulate you both.

CATHERINE: Thank you so much, Desmond.

JOHN: Thank you.

DESMOND: Of course, it's quite expected, I know. Quite expected. Still it was rather a surprise, hearing it like that—from Violet.

CATHERINE: We were going to tell you, Desmond, dear. It was only official this morning, you know. In fact, you're the first person to hear it.

DESMOND: Am I? Am I, indeed? Well, I'm sure you'll both be very happy.

GRACE *comes downstairs.*

GRACE: Hullo, Desmond, dear.

DESMOND: Hullo, Mrs. Winslow.

GRACE: *(To* CATHERINE*)* I've got him to bed—

CATHERINE: Good.

DESMOND: Nobody ill, I hope?

GRACE: No, no. Nothing wrong at all—

ARTHUR *comes in from the backstairs, with bottles under his arm. In the BG we see the* MAID *laying the dining room table.*

ARTHUR: Grace, when did we last have the cellars seen to?

GRACE: I can't remember, dear.

ARTHUR: Well, they're in shocking condition. Hullo, Desmond. How are you? You're not looking well.

DESMOND: Am I not? Threw my shoulder out, you know—

ARTHUR *carries the bottles into the dining room.* JOHN
steers DESMOND *into the drawing room, followed by*
CATHERINE *and* GRACE.

21. INT. WINSLOW DRAWING ROOM. DAY.
JOHN: Are you any relation of D. W. H. Curry who used
    to play for Middlesex?
DESMOND: I am D. W. H. Curry.
GRACE: Didn't you know we had a great man in the room?
JOHN: Curry of Curry's match?
DESMOND: That's right.
ARTHUR *wanders in and rings the bell.*

22. INT. WINSLOW BACKSTAIRS HALLWAY. DAY.

ANGLE. ON VIOLET.
*She is appearing to supervise the laying of the table. She
points to the* MAID *and points down to the floor. The*
MAID *nods and hurries off.*
    The MAID *hurries back with a mop and begins to mop
up the puddle on the spot where* RONNIE *was standing. In
the BG we see and hear* DESMOND *and* JOHN.
JOHN: Hat trick against the Player, in what year was it . . . ?
DESMOND: Eighteen ninety-five at Lords.
JOHN: You were a *hero* of mine.
DESMOND: Was I, was I indeed . . . ?

23. INT. WINSLOW DRAWING ROOM. DAY.
VIOLET *comes in, in response to the bell rung by* ARTHUR
some moments before.
VIOLET: Sir.
ARTHUR: Yes, Violet. Bring some glasses, would you?
VIOLET: Very good, sir.
She goes out. CATHERINE *wraps a shawl around herself.*

ARTHUR: I thought we'd try a little of the Madeira before luncheon—we're celebrating.

GRACE *jogs his arm furtively, indicating* DESMOND.

CATHERINE: It's all right, Father. Desmond knows—

DESMOND: Yes, indeed. It's wonderful news, isn't it? I'll most gladly drink a toast to the—er—to the—

ARTHUR: *(Politely)* Happy pair, I think, is the phrase that is eluding you—

DESMOND: Well, as a matter of fact, I was looking for something new to say—

ARTHUR: *(Murmuring)* A forlorn quest, my dear Desmond.

GRACE: *(Protestingly)* Arthur, really! You mustn't be so rude.

ARTHUR: I meant, naturally, that no one—with the possible exception of Voltaire—could find anything new to say about an engaged couple—

DICKIE *comes in.*

ARTHUR: *(Cont'd.)* Ah, my dear Dickie—just in time for a glass of Madeira in celebration of Kate's engagement.

VIOLET *comes in with a tray of glasses.* ARTHUR *begins to pour out the wine.*

DICKIE: Oh, is that all finally spliced up now? Kate definitely being entered for the marriage stakes. Good egg!

ARTHUR: Quite so. I should have added just now—with the possible exception of Voltaire and Dickie Winslow. *(To Violet)* Take these round, will you, Violet?

VIOLET *goes first to* GRACE, *then to* CATHERINE, *then to* JOHN, DESMOND, DICKIE, *and finally* ARTHUR.

CATHERINE: Are we allowed to drink to our own healths?

ARTHUR: I think it's permissible.

GRACE: No. It's bad luck.

JOHN: We defy augury. Don't we, Kate?

GRACE: You mustn't say that, John dear. I know. You can drink to each other's healths. That's all right.

ARTHUR: There is no Augury in Israel—our superstitious terrors are allayed? Good.

The drinks have now been handed around.

ARTHUR: *(Cont'd. Toasting)* Catherine and John!

*All drink—*CATHERINE *and* JOHN *to each other.* VIOLET *lingers, smiling, in the doorway.*

ARTHUR: *(Cont'd. Seeing Violet)* Ah, Violet. We mustn't leave you out. You must join this toast.

VIOLET: Oh, nothing for me, sir.

He pours her a glass.

VIOLET: *(Cont'd.)* Well, perhaps. Just a sip.

ARTHUR: Quite so. Your reluctance would be more convincing if I hadn't noticed you'd brought an extra glass—

VIOLET: *(Taking glass from* ARTHUR*)* Oh, I didn't bring it for myself, sir. I brought it for Master Ronnie— *(She extends her glass.)* Miss Kate and Mr. John.

ARTHUR: You bought an extra glass for Master Ronnie, Violet?

VIOLET: *(Mistaking his bewilderment)* Well—I thought you might allow him just a taste, sir. Just to drink the toast. He's that grown up these days. *(She turns to go.)*

ARTHUR: Master Ronnie isn't due back from Osbourne until Tuesday, Violet.

VIOLET: Oh no, sir, he's back already. The girl said.

ARTHUR: Christmas holidays don't begin till Tuesday.

VIOLET: Well, the girl saw him with her own two eyes. Isn't that right, mum?

Pause.

ARTHUR: Grace, what does this mean?

CATHERINE: *(Pause)* Alright, Violet, you can go.

VIOLET: Yes, miss.

She goes out.

ARTHUR: *(To* CATHERINE*)* Did *you* know Ronnie was back?

CATHERINE: Yes—

ARTHUR: And you, Dickie?

DICKIE: Yes, Father.

ARTHUR: Grace?

GRACE: *(Pause)* We thought it best you shouldn't know for the time being. Only for the time being, Arthur.

ARTHUR: *(Slowly)* Is the boy very ill?

No one answers. ARTHUR *looks from one face to another.*

ARTHUR: *(Cont'd.)* Answer me, someone. Is the boy very ill? Surely I have the right to know. If he's ill I must be with him—

CATHERINE: *(Steadily)* No, Father. He's not ill.

Pause.

ARTHUR: Will someone tell me what has happened, please?

GRACE *looks at* CATHERINE *with helpless inquiry.* CATHERINE *nods, and hands the letter to her mother.*

GRACE: *(Timidly)* He brought this letter for you—Arthur.

ARTHUR *pats his pockets, looking for his eyeglasses—he cannot find them.*

ARTHUR: Read it to me, please—

GRACE: Arthur—not in front of—

ARTHUR: Read it to me, please.

GRACE *again looks at* CATHERINE *for advice, and again receives a nod.* GRACE *begins to read.*

   As GRACE *reads the letter, intercut are CUs of the family, and an INS. of the letter itself.*

GRACE: *(Reading)* "Confidential. I am commanded by My Lords' Commissioners of the Admiralty to inform you that they have received a communication from the Commanding Officer of the Royal Naval College at Osbourne, reporting the theft of a five-shilling postal order at the College on the seventh instant, which was afterwards cashed at the Post Office. Investigation of the circumstances of the case leaves no other conclusion possible than that the postal order was taken by your son, Cadet Ronald Arthur Winslow. My Lords deeply regret that they must therefore request you to withdraw your son from the College." It's signed by someone—I can't quite read his name—

She turns away quickly. CATHERINE *puts an arm on her shoulder.* ARTHUR *has not changed his attitude. There is a pause, during which we can hear the sound of a gong in the hall outside.*

ARTHUR: *(At length)* Desmond—be so good as to call Violet.

DESMOND *does so. There is another pause, until* VIOLET *comes in.*

VIOLET: Yes, sir.

ARTHUR: Violet, will you ask Master Ronnie to come down and see me, please?

GRACE: Arthur—he's in bed.

ARTHUR: You told me he wasn't ill.

GRACE: He's not at all well.

ARTHUR: Do as I say, please, Violet.

VIOLET: Very good, sir.

She goes out.

ARTHUR: Perhaps the rest of you would go in to luncheon? Grace, would you take them in?

GRACE: Arthur— don't you think—

ARTHUR: Dickie, will you decant the bottle of claret I

brought from the cellar? I put it on the sideboard in
the dining room.

DICKIE: Yes, Father.

He goes out.

ARTHUR: Will you go in, Desmond? And John?

The two men go out toward the dining room in silence.

GRACE *still hovers.*

GRACE: Arthur?

ARTHUR: Yes, Grace?

GRACE: Please don't—please don't— *(She stops, uncer-
tainly.)*

ARTHUR: What mustn't I do?

GRACE: Please don't forget he's only a child.

ARTHUR *does not answer her.* CATHERINE *takes her
mother's arm.*

CATHERINE: Come on, Mother.

She leads her mother toward the dining room. At the door
GRACE *looks back at* ARTHUR. ARTHUR *walks into the
study, closing the doors behind him.*

24. INT. WINSLOW STUDY. DAY.

ARTHUR *picks up his glasses from their place next to the
magnifying glass. He reads the letter.*

HOLD.

*There is the sound of a knock at the door. He lays the let-
ter down.*

ANGLE, ARTHUR'S POV.

RONNIE, *in a bathrobe, stands on the threshold.*

ARTHUR: Come in. *(Pause)* Come in and close the door.

ANGLE. ON THE DOOR.

As RONNIE *enters, camera takes him into the room.*

ARTHUR: *(Cont'd.)* Come over here.

RONNIE *walks slowly to his father.* ARTHUR *gazes at him steadily for some time, without speaking.*

ARTHUR: *(Cont'd. At length)* Why aren't you in uniform?

RONNIE: *(Murmuring)* It got wet.

ARTHUR: How did it get wet?

RONNIE: I was out in the garden in the rain.

ARTHUR: Why?

RONNIE: *(Reluctantly)* I was hiding.

ARTHUR: From me?

RONNIE *nods.*

ARTHUR: *(Cont'd.)* Do you remember once, you promised me that if ever you were in trouble of any sort you would come to me first?

RONNIE: Yes, Father.

ARTHUR: Why didn't you come to me now? Why did you have to go and hide in the garden?

RONNIE: I don't know, Father.

ARTHUR: Are you so frightened of me?

RONNIE *does not reply.* ARTHUR *gazes at him for a moment, then picks up the letter.*

ARTHUR: *(Cont'd.)* In this letter it says you stole a postal order.

RONNIE *opens his mouth to speak.*

ARTHUR: *(Cont'd. Stops him)* No, I don't want you to say a word until you've heard what *I've* got to say. If you did it, you must tell me. I shan't be angry with you, Ronnie—provided you tell me the truth. But if you tell me a lie, I shall know it, because a lie between you and me can't be hidden. I shall know it, Ronnie—so remember that before you speak. *(Pause)* Did you steal this postal order?

RONNIE: *(Without hesitation)* No, Father. I didn't.

ARTHUR: *(Staring into his eyes)* Did you steal this postal order?

RONNIE: No, Father. I didn't.

ARTHUR *continues to stare into his eyes for a second.*

ARTHUR: Go on back to bed.

RONNIE *goes gratefully to the door. He lays down the official envelope.*

ANGLE, INS. HOLDING ON THE OFFICIAL ENVELOPE.
As ARTHUR *slides it and the letter under the magnifying glass.*

DISSOLVE TO:

25. INT. PRINT SHOP. DAY.
A woodstove with a vase of flowers on it. Pan past a window, open, the curtains blowing. A spring day.

A BRAWNY MAN, *wearing a folded newsprint compositor's cap, removes a proof sheet from a press and hands it to a shirtsleeved* EDITOR, *who tacks it on a board and begins making proofreading marks on it with a red pencil. We push in to read.*

"The Osborne Cadet"

The hand of the editor, with the red pencil, inserts a u *in the word* Osbourne.

"Sir, I am entirely in agreement with your correspondent, Democrat, concerning the scandalously high-handed treatment by the Admiralty of the case of the Osbourne Cadet."

The EDITOR's *hand continues making corrections in the sheet. Sound of a railroad train whistle.* EDITOR *takes the corrected sheet from its position on the wall. Screen goes black for a second.*

26. EXT. TUBE PLATFORM. DAY.
Tight two shot, two MEN IN BOWLERS, *one reading a paper, the other reading over his shoulder, the man reading turns the page, the other man cranes his head. One wears a badge saying, "I'm for the Winslow Boy."*

ANGLE, HIS POV. AS THE PAGE TURNS.
It reads: "The Osbourne Cadet. The efforts of Mr. Arthur Winslow to secure a fair trial for his son, having been thwarted at every turn . . ."

27. INT. SUFFRAGETTE OFFICE. DAY.
DICKIE *seated at a desk in the suffragettes' office. Next to him, a young woman* SUFFRAGETTE *(we will see her again in the gallery at the House of Commons) is typing.* DICKIE, *his schoolbooks beside him, reads from a newspaper.*
DICKIE: "Thwarted at every turn by a Soulless Oligarchy." Soulless Oligarchy, that's rather good. "It is high time private and peaceful citizens of this country woke to the increasing encroachments of their ancient freedoms."
SUFFRAGETTE: . . . tell me a piece of news.
She gets up, takes the bit she was typing, and moves farther back into the office, followed by DICKIE *and camera.*
DICKIE: I'll tell you a piece of news. Saw a chap on the train today, had on brown boots. Brown boots, I Arst yer.
SUFFRAGETTE: Did he have on a brown suit?
DICKIE: That doesn't excuse it.
Camera takes them to CATHERINE, *who is sitting in a small semicubicle in front of a suffragette-rage banner.*
SUFFRAGETTE: *(Handing the typed sheet to* CATHERINE*)* Can you get this out by this afternoon?

CATHERINE: I have to go to the Law Library.

The SUFFRAGETTE *walks over to another* SUFFRAGETTE *and asks the same question. The camera stays on* DICKIE *and* CATHERINE.

DICKIE: Fighting on Many fronts, 'z 'at it, Cath?

CATHERINE: Yes, that's right, darling . . .

DICKIE: "Cannon to the Right of you," 'n' so on . . . ?

CATHERINE: . . . mmm.

DICKIE: They paying you here yet?

CATHERINE: No, I just do it for the sport of the thing.

DICKIE *picks up the newspaper again, and reads.*

DICKIE: The other's from Perplexed. "What with the present troubles in the Balkans, and the further inquiry at which the Judge Advocate of the Fleet confirmed the findings that the boy was *Guilty* . . . dah, dah, dah . . . This correspondence now must cease."

He lays down the newspaper.

ANGLE, INS.

The paper reads, "This correspondence now must cease."

ANGLE.

They walk to the door.

DICKIE: *(Cont'd.)* You know, but I rather see Perplexed's point. Well *(Pause)* 'n any case, it will blow over, before the wedding. *(Pause. He looks at her.)* Postponed again?

CATHERINE: His father's out of the country.

DICKIE: Nothing wrong? I mean, I'm not going to have to "quirt him with my riding crop," am I . . . as he comes out of his Club?

CATHERINE: This correspondence now must cease.

She pins a suffrage button on his coat.

DICKIE: Oh, Lord, late f'ra meeting with the guv . . .

28. INT. BANK LOBBY. DAY.

Several men and women banking. Camera follows DICKIE
as he enters the bank, carrying his books. He approaches a
CASHIER, *who looks up from his books.*

CASHIER: May I help you . . . ?

Recognizing DICKIE, *he nods him through a wooden door
behind him and heads him into a corridor.*

29. ANGLE, INT. ARTHUR WINSLOW'S OFFICE. DAY.

A small, neat, wood-paneled room. As DICKIE *enters,*
ARTHUR *rises. A* BANK OFFICER *and* CLERK *leave.*

ARTHUR: Would you close the door, please?

DICKIE *does so. There is a tray of coffee on the table, and
a fire behind* ARTHUR's *desk.*

ARTHUR: *(Cont'd.)* I must ask you a question. But before I
   do I must impress on you the urgent necessity for an
   absolutely truthful answer.

DICKIE: Naturally.

ARTHUR: *Naturally* means "by nature," and I am afraid I
   have not yet noticed that it has invariably been your
   nature to answer my questions truthfully.

DICKIE: Oh. Well, I will this one, Father, I promise.

ARTHUR: Very well. *(He stares at* DICKIE *for a moment.)*
   What do you suppose one of your bookmaker friends
   would lay in the way of odds against your getting a
   degree?

Pause.

DICKIE: Oh. Well, let's think. Say—about evens.

ARTHUR: Hm. I rather doubt that if at that price your
   friend would find many takers.

DICKIE: Well—perhaps seven to four against.

ARTHUR: I see. And what about the odds against your
   eventually becoming a Civil Servant?

DICKIE: Well—a bit steeper, I suppose.

ARTHUR: Exactly. Quite a bit steeper.

Pause.

DICKIE: You don't want to have a bet, do you?

ARTHUR: No, Dickie. I'm not a gambler. And that's exactly the trouble. Unhappily I'm no longer in a position to gamble two hundred pounds a year on what you yourself admit is an outside chance.

DICKIE: Not an outside chance, Father. A good chance. It's the case, I suppose.

ARTHUR: It's costing me a lot of money—

DICKIE: I know. I must be—still, couldn't you . . . I mean, isn't there a way . . . ?

ARTHUR: Not good enough, Dickie. I'm afraid—with things as they are at the moment. Definitely not good enough. I fear my mind is finally made up.

There is a long pause.

DICKIE: You want me to leave Oxford—is that it?

ARTHUR: I'm very much afraid so, Dickie.

DICKIE: Oh. Straight away?

ARTHUR: No. You can finish your second year.

DICKIE: And then what?

ARTHUR: I can get you a job here in the bank.

DICKIE: *(Quietly)* Oh, Lord!

Pause.

ARTHUR: *(Rather apologetically)* It'll be quite a good job, you know. Luckily my influence here still counts for something.

DICKIE: *(Getting up)* Father—if I promised you—I mean, really promised you—I mean, isn't there any way—

ARTHUR *again shakes his head slowly.*

DICKIE: *(Cont'd.)* Oh, Lord!

ARTHUR: I'm afraid this is rather a shock for you. I'm sorry.

DICKIE: What? No. No, it isn't really. I've been rather expecting it, as a matter of fact . . . Things . . . things are tight.

ARTHUR: Yes. "Things are tight."

DICKIE: And you're, um, still hoping, still hoping to brief Sir Robert Morton.

ARTHUR: We're hoping.

DICKIE: *That'd* take a bit of tin—

ARTHUR: Yes. It would, Son.

DICKIE: *(Pause)* Ah ha. Still . . . still, I can't say but what it isn't a bit of a slap in the face.

Pause.

ARTHUR *looks at his watch.*

ARTHUR: There is a journalist coming to see me. Perhaps you would see me to a cab.

DICKIE: Of course, Father.

DICKIE *begins to gather his books.*

ARTHUR: *(With a half smile)* I should leave those there, if I were you.

DICKIE: Yes. Thank you. Good idea.

ARTHUR *picks up a walking stick and starts for the door.*

ARTHUR: I must thank you, Dickie, for bearing what must have been a very unpleasant blow with some fortitude.

DICKIE: Oh. Rot, Father.

DISSOLVE TO:

30. INT. WINSLOW HALLWAY. DAY.
Shot over a cream-colored envelope on a hall stand, as ARTHUR, *followed by* MISS BARNES, *a journalist, and* FRED, *a photographer, enters the house.*

31. INT. WINSLOW STUDY/DRAWING ROOM. DAY.
*Camera takes them into the study, now turned into a
study/war room. Pans over books titled* Maritime Law,
The Admiralty and the Civil Courts, *et cetera.*

MISS BARNES: *(VO)* My paper usually sends me out on stories which have a special appeal to women—stories
with a little heart, you know, like this one—a father's
fight for his little boy's honor—

ARTHUR: *(VO)* I venture to think this case has rather wider
implications than that—

*He moves to his desk, opens mail and peruses it, as they
speak.*

ARTHUR: *(Cont'd. To* MISS BARNES*)* Forgive me . . .

*He hunts in his desk for his glasses, which are next to the
magnifying glass, under which is the old letter from
Osbourne.*

MISS BARNES: Oh, yes. Now, what I'd really like to do
is to get a nice picture of you and your little boy
together.

ARTHUR: My son is arriving from school in a few minutes.
His mother has gone to the station to meet him.

MISS BARNES: *(Making a note)* From school? How interesting. So you got a school to take him? I mean, they
didn't mind the unpleasantness?

ARTHUR: No.

MISS BARNES: And why is he coming back this time?

ARTHUR: He hasn't been expelled again, if that is what
you're implying. He is coming to London to be exam-
ined by Sir Robert Morton, whom we are hoping to
brief—

MISS BARNES: But do you *really* think he'll take a little case
like this?

ARTHUR: It is *not* a little case, madam—

MISS BARNES: No, no. Of course not. *(Pause)* Well, now, perhaps you wouldn't mind giving me a few details. When did it all start?

ARTHUR: *(Puts on his glasses and hunts in his desk for papers. VO)* Nine months ago. The first I knew of the charge was when my son arrived home with a letter from the Admiralty informing me of his expulsion. I telephoned Osbourne to protest and was referred by them to the Lords of the Admiralty. My solicitors then took the matter up. We applied to the Admiralty for a Court-Martial. They ignored us. We applied for a civil trial. They ignored us again.

MISS BARNES: . . . yes.

ARTHUR: Yes. But after the tremendous pressure had been brought to bear—letters to the papers, questions in the House, and other means open to private citizens of this country—the Admiralty eventually agreed to what they called an independent inquiry.

MISS BARNES: Oh, good!

ARTHUR: It was not good, madam. At that independent inquiry, conducted by the Judge Advocate of the Fleet, against whom I am saying nothing, mind you, my son, a child of fourteen, was not represented by counsel, solicitors, or friends. What do you think of that?

MISS BARNES: Fancy!

ARTHUR: You may well say "fancy."

MISS BARNES: And what happened at that inquiry?

ARTHUR: What do you think happened? Inevitably he was found guilty again, and thus branded for the second time before the world as a thief and a forger—

MISS BARNES: What a shame!

ARTHUR: I need hardly tell you, madam, that I am not prepared to let the matter rest there. I shall continue to fight this monstrous injustice with every weapon and every means at my disposal. Now, it happens I have a plan—I have approached, I might say "petitioned," Sir Robert . . .

MISS BARNES: Oh, what charming curtains! What are they made of?

She rises and goes to the drawing room window. ARTHUR *sits for a moment in paralyzed silence.*

ARTHUR: *(At last)* Madam—I fear I have no idea.

There is the sound of voices in the hall.

MISS BARNES: Ah. Do I hear the poor little chap himself?

She moves into the hallway. ARTHUR *follows.*

32. INT. WINSLOW HALLWAY. DAY.

ANGLE. OVER THE CREAM-COLORED ENVELOPE.

The hall door opens, and RONNIE *comes in boisterously, followed by* GRACE. *He is evidently in the highest of spirits.*

RONNIE: Hullo, Father!

He runs to him.

ARTHUR: Hullo, Ronnie.

RONNIE: I say, Father! Mr. Moore says I'm to tell you I needn't come back until Monday if you like. So that gives me three whole days.

ARTHUR: Mind my leg!

RONNIE: Sorry, Father.

ARTHUR: How are you, my boy?

RONNIE: Oh, I'm absolutely tophole, Father. Mother says I've grown an inch—

MISS BARNES: Ah! Now that's exactly the way I'd like to take my picture. Would you hold it, Mr. Winslow? Fred! Come in now, will you?

RONNIE: *(In a sibilant whisper)* Who's she?

FRED: Afternoon, all. *(To* MISS BARNES*)* . . . losing the
   light, miss . . .

MISS BARNES: Yes. I was . . . might we go to the *Park* . . . ?
   (To GRACE*)* Do you know, do you know, I was *think-
   ing,* might we go to the *Park,* do you think? *(To* RON-
   NIE*)* You could put on your *uniform* . . .

ARTHUR: No, I don't . . .

MISS BARNES: Something to stress his *youth,* then, his,
   d'you have any *cricket* clothes . . . ?

ARTHUR: Grace, dear, this lady is from the *Beacon.* She is
   extremely interested in your curtains.

GRACE: Oh, really, how nice.

MISS BARNES: Yes, indeed, I was wondering what they
   were made of.

GRACE: Well, it's an entirely new material, you know. I'm
   afraid I don't know what it's called, but I got them at
   Barker's last year. Apparently it's a sort of mixture of
   wild silk and—

FRED: Losing the light, miss.

MISS BARNES: If we could, do you see, put him in Cricket
   Costume, d'you see? Something which would say,
   both *England,* and *Youth.*

ARTHUR: Alright.

FRED: *(Picking up his apparatus)* I'm going to set up.

MISS BARNES: Yes, and can you come along *quickly,* do
   you see, if we are going to get this picture.

GRACE: Yes. *(To* RONNIE*)* We'll meet you in the Park . . .
   *She rummages in the hall stand. We see, in the FG, the
   cream-colored envelope.*

GRACE: *(Cont'd.)* . . . I found the Name of the Material.

MISS BARNES: Good-bye, Mr. Winslow. And the very best
   of good fortune in your inspiring fight. It was good of
   you to talk to me, and I'm sure our Readers will be
   most interested.

GRACE *shows her out the front door.*

RONNIE: What's she talking about?

ARTHUR: The case, I imagine.

RONNIE: Oh, the case. Father, do you know the train had fourteen coaches?

ARTHUR: Did it indeed?

RONNIE: Yes. All corridor.

ARTHUR: Remarkable.

RONNIE: Of course, it was one of the very biggest expresses. I walked all the way down it from one end to the other.

ARTHUR: I had your half-term report, Ronnie.

RONNIE: *(Suddenly silenced by perturbation)* Oh, yes?

ARTHUR: On the whole it was pretty fair.

RONNIE: Oh, good.

ARTHUR: I'm glad you seem to be settling down so well.

RONNIE: Yes, thank you, Father. I say, do you know how long the train took? One hundred and twenty-three miles in two hours and fifty-two minutes. That's an average of forty-six point seventy-three miles an hour. I worked it out.

ARTHUR: Worked it out well. Hadn't you better change for the photo——

RONNIE: Oh, yes. Violet! Violet. I'm back!

ARTHUR: *(Calling after him)* . . . she's out.

RONNIE: Will you tell her I'm back?

ARTHUR: You need to go and change.

RONNIE *disappears upstairs.*

   CAMERA *brings* CATHERINE *from the backstairs. She is carrying books. She goes to the study.* ARTHUR *follows.*

33. INT. WINSLOW STUDY/HALLWAY. DAY.

CATHERINE: I take it Ronnie's back, judging by the noise . . . I found a new citation in the Law Library.

She leaves her coat draped over the back banister. Camera takes her into the main hall, into the dining room, which is now strewn with law books, and into the hall, where she looks in the mirror.

ARTHUR: New frock?

CATHERINE: Bless you. I've turned the cuffs.

Pause.

ARTHUR: *(To himself)* . . . turned the cuffs . . .

CATHERINE: . . . what?

ARTHUR: I said, I like your frock.

CATHERINE *moves into the study carrying a book she picked up in the dining room.*

CATHERINE: Like it, it?

ARTHUR: Yes.

CATHERINE: Like it, eh? Hope John likes it. *(She glances at her watch.)*

ANGLE. CATHERINE AND ARTHUR.

CATHERINE *has moved into the study.* RONNIE *runs down the stairs in cricket clothes.* CATHERINE *looks at him and then down again to her book.*

ARTHUR: Kate. Are we both mad? You and I?

She takes out a book and opens it. On the desk we see a piece of sheet music, a picture of RONNIE, *in an admiral's hat, on a ship, sword fighting with a group of admirals on another toy ship, and holding them off. The title is "How, Still, We See Thee Lie, or The Naughty Cadet."*

CATHERINE: *(Sitting near him)* . . . tell me.

ARTHUR: Dress him in Cricket Clothes. To say both Youth and England. A Father's Fight for His Little Boy's Honor. Special Appeal to All Women. Photo Inset of Mrs. Winslow's Curtains. *(Pause)* Shall we drop the whole thing, Kate?

CATHERINE: I didn't hear you.

ARTHUR: Shall we drop the whole thing?

CATHERINE: I don't consider that a serious question.

ANGLE.

CATHERINE *walks out of the study toward the dining room.* ARTHUR *follows and stands in the hallway.*

34. INT. WINSLOW DINING ROOM/HALLWAY. DAY.

CATHERINE *takes a book off the dining room table. She leafs through it, making notes.*

ANGLE, INS. THE BOOK.

We read: Admiralty Law, *vol. 2.*

ARTHUR: . . . you realize that your marriage settlement must go . . . ?

CATHERINE: *(Lightly)* Oh, yes. I gave that up for lost weeks ago.

ARTHUR: Things are all right between you and John, aren't they?

CATHERINE: Oh, yes, Father, of course. Everything's perfect.

ARTHUR: I mean—it won't make any difference to you, will it?

CATHERINE: Good heavens, no!

ARTHUR: Very well, then, Let us pin our faith on the appearance of a champion.

CATHERINE *is silent.* ARTHUR *looks at her as if he had expected an answer, then nods.*

CATHERINE: *(Lightly)* You know what I think of Sir Robert Morton, Father. Don't let's go into it again, now.

ARTHUR: I want the best—

CATHERINE: The best in this case is not Morton.

ARTHUR: Then why does everyone say he is?

CATHERINE: If one happens to be a large monopoly attacking a Trade Union, he's your lad. But it utterly defeats me how you or anyone else could expect a man of his record to have the compassion . . .

VIOLET *passes the door with several packages.*

CATHERINE: *(Cont'd.)* . . . did Mr. *Watherstone* call, Violet?

VIOLET: I'm sorry, miss, I just stepped out, but to the best of my knowledge nobody has c——

CATHERINE: Thank you.

ARTHUR: Well, I imagine, if his heart isn't in it, he won't accept the brief.

CATHERINE: He might still. It depends what there is in it for him. Luckily there isn't much—

ARTHUR: There is a fairly substantial cheque—

CATHERINE: He doesn't want money. He must be a very rich man.

ARTHUR: What does he want, then?

CATHERINE: That which advances his interests.

ARTHUR: *(Shrugs his shoulders)* I believe you are prejudiced because he spoke against woman's suffrage.

CATHERINE: I am. I'm prejudiced because he is always speaking against what is right and just.

At the sound of the telephone CATHERINE *starts up but composes herself as we see* VIOLET, *in the BG, go to the phone in the hall.*

VIOLET: *(Into the phone)* The Winslow residence . . .

CATHERINE *rises and starts toward the phone.*

VIOLET: *(Cont'd. To phone)* Yes, sir . . . *(She hands the phone to* CATHERINE.*)* It's Mr. *Curry,* miss . . .

CATHERINE: . . . Mr. *Curry* . . . ? *(She takes the phone.)* Hello. Hello, Desmond. Yes? *(Pause)* What? We . . .

what? *Violet* . . . did we receive a letter from Mr.
Curry . . . ?

*She looks around and sees the cream-colored envelope on
the hall stand. She picks it up and reads, as she listens to*
DESMOND.

CATHERINE: *(Cont'd.)* Yes, I just . . . *now?* Yes. Yes.
We'll . . . yes, of course. Thank you. *(She hangs up
the telephone.)*

ANGLE, INS. THE NOTE.
We read: ". . . has graciously agreed . . ."

ANGLE. CATHERINE AS SHE RACES UPSTAIRS.

CATHERINE: *(Cont'd.)* Violet. Please ring up a cab.

VIOLET: For when, miss?

CATHERINE: For right now. *(Calling back over her shoulder) Two* cabs. Please . . .

VIOLET *starts calling for the cabs.* CATHERINE *reappears
down the stairs.*

CATHERINE: *(Cont'd. To her father, as she hands him the
piece of paper)* Desmond's got us an appointment
with . . .

*He looks at the piece of paper, looks at his watch. He gets
up and grabs his cane.* VIOLET *is on the phone to the cab
company.* CATHERINE *helps her father to his hat.*

ARTHUR: We will go on ahead. *(To Violet)* You tell the second cab to *wait,* go find Mrs. Winslow and Ronnie in
the Park, he is to *change,* and they are to *meet* us at
the chambers of Sir Robert Morton *immediately* . . .
(He takes the letter from CATHERINE.) Here is the . . .
(He glances at her.)

CATHERINE: I have the address.

ARTHUR: *Immediately* . . . The Chambers of Sir Robert
Morton . . .

CATHERINE *opens the door.*

35. EXT. THE TEMPLE. DAY.
DESMOND CURRY *standing, impatiently, on a street corner,*
looking at his watch.
   A Caticab pulls up, CATHERINE *exits, and she and*
DESMOND *help out* ARTHUR.
DESMOND: We only have . . .
CATHERINE: I'm sorry that we didn't get your note . . .
DESMOND: He has an important, a *most* important dinner
      engagement . . . *(He looks around.)*
ARTHUR: He's coming separately. He'll be here momentar-
      ily, with his mmm——
DESMOND *begins to move them into the building. He*
looks at his watch and frowns.
DESMOND: I'm afraid he can only spare us a very few
      moments of his most valuable time, I . . .
CATHERINE: I assure you, we're most conscious of it . . .
They move ahead, at the pace of ARTHUR, *walking with*
his stick.
CATHERINE: *(Cont'd.)* I'll go ahead . . .
She glances at the note, hurries forward.

36. ANGLE. INT. THE TEMPLE. DAY.
CATHERINE *hurrying up a flight of stairs. She glances at the*
note, then hurries down a corridor and up another flight
of stairs. A group of PEOPLE *emerge from a lawyer's office,*
talking. She pushes through them.

ANGLE, CATHERINE'S POV.
She slides past a weeping young WOMAN, *being comforted*
by a LAWYER.

ANGLE. CATHERINE, CONTINUING TO HURRY DOWN THE
CORRIDOR.

37. INT. MICHAEL'S OFFICE/SIR ROBERT'S CHAMBER.
DAY.

A clerk, MICHAEL, *putting away some papers as he talks on the telephone. He looks up as the door opens.* CATHERINE *enters, meets the clerk's gaze.*

CATHERINE: Miss Catherine Winslow. The Winslow
    Case . . .

MICHAEL: *(Glancing at his watch)* Yes. We understood . . .

CATHERINE: They're coming . . . we didn't hear of . . .

ANGLE.

On SIR ROBERT *in his dressing area, smoking a cigar and getting into his evening wear. He comes forward into his office.* CATHERINE *and* MICHAEL *are beyond.*

ANGLE.

On CATHERINE, *as she turns to see* SIR ROBERT *coming out of his dressing room.*

CATHERINE: I am Catherine Winslow.

SIR ROBERT MORTON: *(Retreating into his dressing area)* I
    beg your pardon . . .

Pause.

   Hold on CATHERINE *and cover on* SIR ROBERT, *as he continues dressing and can see* CATHERINE *through his mirror.*

CATHERINE: I suppose you know the history of this case,
    do you, Sir Robert?

SIR ROBERT MORTON: *(Examining his nails)* I believe I
    have seen most of the relevant documents.

CATHERINE: Do you think we can bring the case into
    Court by a collusive action?

SIR ROBERT MORTON: I really have no idea—

CATHERINE: Curry and Curry seem to think that might
    hold . . .

SIR ROBERT *emerges from his dressing room fastening his cutaway coat. He goes into* MICHAEL's *office.*

SIR ROBERT MORTON: Do they? They are a very reliable firm. *(Extends his hand)* Sir Robert Morton.

CATHERINE: Catherine Winslow.

MICHAEL *hands him a cigarette case and a watch, then presents him several papers, which he signs.*

SIR ROBERT MORTON: *(Of cigarette)* I hope you don't . . .

CATHERINE: What could be more absurd than your asking me permission to smoke in your establishment?

SIR ROBERT MORTON: Well, it is the custom.

CATHERINE: I indulge *myself.*

SIR ROBERT MORTON: Indeed.

CATHERINE: Some people find that shocking.

SIR ROBERT MORTON: Amazing how little it takes, to offend the world's sensibilities.

Pause.

CATHERINE: My father and brother will be here momentarily. *(Pause)*

MICHAEL *brings* SIR ROBERT *a small "Order" in a sewing case.* SIR ROBERT *takes a moment, then takes it and affixes it to his lapel.*

CATHERINE: *(Cont'd.)* What time are you dining?

SIR ROBERT MORTON: Eight o'clock.

CATHERINE: Far from here?

SIR ROBERT MORTON: Devonshire House.

CATHERINE: Oh. Then of course you mustn't on any account be late.

SIR ROBERT MORTON: No.

Pause, as SIR ROBERT *studies the documents* MICHAEL *puts in front of him.*

CATHERINE: I'm rather surprised that a case of this sort should interest you, Sir Robert.

SIR ROBERT MORTON: Are you?

CATHERINE: It seems such a very trivial affair, compared to most of your great forensic triumphs. *(Pause)* I was in Court during your prosecution of Len Rogers, in the Trades Union embezzlement case.

SIR ROBERT MORTON: Really?

CATHERINE: Magnificently done.

SIR ROBERT MORTON: Thank you.

CATHERINE: I suppose you heard that he committed suicide a few months ago?

SIR ROBERT MORTON: Yes, I had heard.

CATHERINE: Many people believed him innocent, you know.

SIR ROBERT MORTON: So I understand. *(Pause)* As it happens, however, he was guilty.

38. INT. SIR ROBERT MORTON'S CHAMBERS/ANTEROOM. DAY.

ARTHUR *and* DESMOND *are shown in.* MICHAEL *leads them into* SIR ROBERT'S *office.*

DESMOND: Sir Robert . . .

ARTHUR: Sir Robert. So sorry to've kept you waiting. So sorry. My . . .

DESMOND: Arthur Winslow . . .

ARTHUR: Sir Robert . . . We didn't get your note . . .

SIR ROBERT MORTON: It's perfectly alright. How do you do?

CATHERINE: Sir Robert is dining at Devonshire House.

The phone rings. MICHAEL *goes to the phone.*

ARTHUR: Yes. Yes. I see. I know that you are pressed for time. My son will be along at any moment. I assume you will want to examine him.

SIR ROBERT MORTON: Just a few questions. I fear that is all I will have time for this evening.

ARTHUR: I am rather sorry. He has made the journey from school especially in hope of this interview, and I had hoped that by the end of it I should know definitely yes or no, if you would accept the brief.

DESMOND: Well, perhaps Sir Robert would consent to finish his examination some other time.

MICHAEL *enters with several papers, which he presents to* SIR ROBERT.

SIR ROBERT MORTON: It might be arranged. *(Of papers)* You'll pardon me . . . ?

ARTHUR: Tomorrow?

SIR ROBERT MORTON: Tomorrow is impossible. I am in Court all the morning and in the House of Commons for the rest of the day.

SIR ROBERT *makes a note and hands it to* MICHAEL.
   Pause.

ARTHUR: I see. Will you forgive me if I sit down? Curry has been telling me you think it might be possible to proceed by Petition of Right.

CATHERINE: What's a Petition of Right?

DESMOND: Well—granting the assumption that the Admiralty, as the Crown, can do no wrong—

CATHERINE: I thought that was exactly the assumption we refused to grant.

DESMOND: In law, I mean. Now, a subject can sue the Crown, nevertheless, by Petition of Right, redress being granted as a matter of grace—and the custom is for the Attorney General—on behalf of the King—to endorse the Petition, and allow the case to come to Court.

SIR ROBERT MORTON: It is interesting to note that the

exact words he uses on such occasions are: Let Right
be done.

ARTHUR: Let Right be done? I like that phrase, sir.

SIR ROBERT MORTON: It has a certain ring about it, has it
not? *(Languidly)* Let Right be done.

39. INT. SIR ROBERT MORTON'S CHAMBERS. DAY.

SIR ROBERT *finishes with the papers.* MICHAEL *nods and
retires a step as the door opens and* GRACE *and* RONNIE
enter. RONNIE *is dressed in an Eton suit.*

ARTHUR: Grace, Sir Robert Morton, this is Mrs. Winslow,
and this is my son, Ronnie. *(Pause)* Ronnie, Sir
Robert Morton.

RONNIE: How do you do, sir?

ARTHUR: He is going to ask you a few questions. You must
answer them all truthfully—as you always have. *(He
begins to struggle out of his chair.)* I expect you
would like us to leave—

SIR ROBERT MORTON: No, provided, of course, that you
don't interrupt. *(To* CATHERINE*)* Miss Winslow, will
you sit down, please?

CATHERINE *takes a seat.*

SIR ROBERT MORTON *(Cont'd. To* RONNIE*)* Will you stand
at the table, facing me?

RONNIE *does so.*

SIR ROBERT MORTON: *(Cont'd.)* That's right.

SIR ROBERT *and* RONNIE *now face each other across the
table.* SIR ROBERT *begins his examination very quietly.*

SIR ROBERT MORTON: *(Cont'd.)* Now, Ronald, how old are
you?

RONNIE: Fourteen and seven months.

SIR ROBERT MORTON: You were, then, thirteen and ten
months old when you left Osbourne: is that right?

RONNIE: Yes, sir.

SIR ROBERT MORTON: Now I would like to cast your mind back to July seventh of last year. Will you tell me in your own words exactly what happened to you on that day?

RONNIE: All right. Well, it was a half holiday, so we didn't have any work after dinner—

SIR ROBERT MORTON: Dinner? At one o'clock?

RONNIE: Yes. At least, until prep at seven.

SIR ROBERT MORTON: Prep at seven?

RONNIE: Just before dinner I went to the Chief Petty Officer and asked him to let me have fifteen and six out of what I had in the school bank—

SIR ROBERT MORTON: Why did you do that?

RONNIE: I wanted to buy an air pistol.

SIR ROBERT MORTON: Which cost fifteen and six?

RONNIE: Yes, sir.

SIR ROBERT MORTON: And how much money did you have in the school bank at the time?

RONNIE: Two pounds, three shillings.

ARTHUR: So you see, sir, what incentive could there possibly be for him to steal five shillings?

SIR ROBERT MORTON: I must ask you to be good enough not to interrupt me, sir. *(To* RONNIE*)* After you had withdrawn the fifteen and six, what did you do?

RONNIE: I had dinner.

SIR ROBERT MORTON: Then what?

RONNIE: I went to the locker room and put the fifteen and six in my locker.

SIR ROBERT MORTON: Yes. Then?

RONNIE: I went to get permission to go down to the Post Office. Then I went to the locker room, again got out my money, and went down to the Post Office.

SIR ROBERT MORTON: I see. Go on.

RONNIE: I bought my postal order—

SIR ROBERT MORTON: For fifteen and six?

RONNIE: Yes. Then I went back to College. Then I met Elliot Minor, and he said: "I say, isn't it rot? Someone's broken into my locker and pinched a postal order. I've reported it to the P.O."

SIR ROBERT MORTON: Those were Elliot Minor's exact words?

RONNIE: He might have used another word for *rot*—

SIR ROBERT MORTON: I see. Continue—

RONNIE: Well, then just before prep I was told to go along and see Commander Flower. The woman from the Post Office was there, and the Commander said, "Is this the boy?" And she said: "It might be. I can't be sure. They all look so much alike."

ARTHUR: You see? She couldn't identify him.

SIR ROBERT MORTON: *(To RONNIE)* Go on.

RONNIE: Then she said: "I only know that the boy who bought a postal order for fifteen and six was the same boy that cashed one for five shillings." So the Commander said: "Did you buy a postal order for fifteen and six?" And I said: "Yes," and then they made me write Elliot Minor's name on an envelope, and compared it to the signature on the postal order—then they sent me to the sanatorium, and ten days later I was sacked—I mean—expelled.

SIR ROBERT MORTON: I see. *(Quietly)* Did you cash a postal order belonging to Elliot Minor for five shillings?

RONNIE: No, sir.

SIR ROBERT MORTON: Did you break into his locker and steal it?

RONNIE: No, sir.

SIR ROBERT MORTON: And that is the truth, the whole truth, and nothing but the truth?

A UNIFORMED CHAUFFEUR *has come into the chambers and stands, by* MICHAEL, *in the BG.*

RONNIE: Yes, sir.

SIR ROBERT MORTON: Right. When the Commander asked you to write Elliot's name on an envelope, how did you write it? With Christian name or initials?

RONNIE: I wrote Charles K. Elliot.

SIR ROBERT MORTON: Charles K. Elliot. Did you by any chance happen to see the forged postal order in the Commander's office?

RONNIE: Oh, yes. The Commander showed it to me.

SIR ROBERT MORTON: Before or after you had written Elliot's name on the envelope?

RONNIE: After.

SIR ROBERT MORTON: After. And did you happen to see how Elliot's name was written on the postal order?

RONNIE: Yes, sir. The same.

SIR ROBERT MORTON: The same? Charles K. Elliot?

RONNIE: Yes, sir.

SIR ROBERT MORTON: When you wrote on the envelope, what made you choose that particular form?

RONNIE: That was the way he usually signed his name—

SIR ROBERT MORTON: How did you know?

RONNIE: Well—he was a great friend of mine—

SIR ROBERT MORTON: That is no answer. How did you know?

RONNIE: I'd seen him sign things.

SIR ROBERT MORTON: What things?

RONNIE: Oh—ordinary things.

SIR ROBERT MORTON: I repeat: what things?

RONNIE: *(Reluctantly)* Bits of paper.

SIR ROBERT MORTON: Bits of paper? And why did he sign his name on bits of paper?

RONNIE: He was practicing his signature.

SIR ROBERT MORTON: And you saw him?

RONNIE: Yes.

SIR ROBERT MORTON: Did he know you saw him?

RONNIE: Well—yes—

SIR ROBERT MORTON: In other words, he showed you exactly how he wrote his signature?

RONNIE: Yes. I suppose he did.

SIR ROBERT MORTON: Did you practice writing it yourself?

RONNIE: I might have done.

SIR ROBERT MORTON: What do you mean, you might have done? Did you or did you not?

RONNIE: Yes—

ARTHUR: Ronnie! You never told me that.

RONNIE: It was only for a joke—

SIR ROBERT MORTON: Never mind if it was for a joke or not. The fact is you practiced forging Elliot's signature—

RONNIE: It wasn't forging—

SIR ROBERT MORTON: What do you call it then?

RONNIE: Writing.

SIR ROBERT MORTON: Very well. Writing. Whoever stole the postal order and cashed it also *wrote* Elliot's signature, didn't he?

RONNIE: Yes.

SIR ROBERT MORTON: And, oddly enough, in the exact form in which you had earlier been practicing *writing* his signature.

RONNIE: I say. Which side are you on?

MICHAEL: Are you *aware* . . .

MICHAEL *takes a piece of paper from a folder and starts to hand it to* SIR ROBERT. SIR ROBERT *waves it off, to say,* "Yes, I know what it contains."

MICHAEL: *(Cont'd.)* Are you aware that the Admiralty sent up the forged postal order to Mr. Ridgely-Pearce, the greatest handwriting expert in England?

RONNIE: Yes.

MICHAEL: *(Showing blown-up handwriting samples)* . . . you *are* aware of that . . . And you know that Mr. Ridgely-Pearce affirmed that there was no doubt that the signature on the postal order and the signature you wrote on the envelope were by one and the same hand?

RONNIE: Yes.

MICHAEL: And you still say you didn't forge that signature?

RONNIE: Yes, I do.

MICHAEL: In other words, Mr. Ridgely-Pearce doesn't know his job?

RONNIE: Well, he's wrong anyway.

SIR ROBERT MORTON: When you went into the locker room after dinner, were you alone?

RONNIE: I don't remember.

SIR ROBERT MORTON: I think you do. Were you alone in the locker room?

RONNIE: Yes.

SIR ROBERT MORTON: And you knew which was Elliot's locker?

RONNIE: Yes. Of course.

SIR ROBERT MORTON: Why did you go in there at all?

RONNIE: I've told you. To put my fifteen and six away.

SIR ROBERT MORTON: Why?

RONNIE: I thought it would be safer.

SIR ROBERT MORTON: Why safer than your pocket?

RONNIE: I don't know.

SIR ROBERT MORTON: You had it in your pocket at dinner-time. Why the sudden fear for its safety?

RONNIE: I tell you, I don't know—

SIR ROBERT MORTON: It was rather an odd thing to do, wasn't it? The money was perfectly safe in your pocket. Why did you suddenly feel yourself impelled to put it away in your locker?

RONNIE: I don't know.

SIR ROBERT MORTON: Was it because you knew you would be alone in the locker room at that time?

RONNIE: No.

SIR ROBERT MORTON: Where was Elliot's locker in relation to yours?

RONNIE: Next to it, but one.

SIR ROBERT MORTON: Next, but one. What time did Elliot put his postal order in his locker?

RONNIE: I don't know. I didn't even know he had a postal order at all—

SIR ROBERT MORTON: Yet you say he was a great friend of yours—

RONNIE: He didn't tell me he had one.

SIR ROBERT MORTON: How very secretive of him. What time did you go to the locker room?

RONNIE: I don't remember.

SIR ROBERT MORTON: Was it directly after dinner?

RONNIE: Yes, I think so.

SIR ROBERT MORTON: What did you do after leaving the locker room?

RONNIE: I've told you. I went for permission to go to the Post Office.

SIR ROBERT MORTON: What time was that?

RONNIE: About a quarter past two.

SIR ROBERT MORTON: Dinner is over at a quarter to two. Which means that you were in the locker room for half an hour?

RONNIE: I wasn't there all that time—

SIR ROBERT MORTON: How long were you there?

RONNIE: About five minutes.

SIR ROBERT MORTON: What were you doing for the other twenty-five?

RONNIE: I don't remember.

SIR ROBERT MORTON: It's odd that your memory is so good about some things and so bad about others—

RONNIE: Perhaps I waited outside the C.O.'s office.

SIR ROBERT MORTON: Perhaps you waited outside the C.O.'s office! And perhaps no one saw you there either?

RONNIE: No. I don't think they did.

SIR ROBERT MORTON: What were you thinking about outside the C.O.'s office for twenty-five minutes?

RONNIE: I don't even know if I was there. I can't remember. Perhaps I wasn't there at all.

SIR ROBERT MORTON: No. Perhaps you were still in the locker room rifling Elliot's locker—

ARTHUR: Sir Robert, I must ask you—

SIR ROBERT MORTON: Quiet!

RONNIE: I remember now. I remember. Someone did see me outside the C.O.'s office. A chap called Casey. I remember I spoke to him.

SIR ROBERT MORTON: What did you say?

RONNIE: I said: "Come down to the Post Office with me. I'm going to cash a postal order."

SIR ROBERT MORTON: *Cash* a postal order.

RONNIE: I mean *get*.

SIR ROBERT MORTON: You said *cash*. Why did you say *cash* if you meant *get*?

RONNIE: I don't know.

SIR ROBERT MORTON: I suggest *cash* was the truth.

RONNIE: No, no. It wasn't. It wasn't really. You're muddling me.

SIR ROBERT MORTON: You seem easily muddled. How
many other lies have you told?

RONNIE: None. Really, I haven't—

SIR ROBERT MORTON: I suggest your whole testimony is a
lie—

RONNIE: No! It's the truth—

SIR ROBERT MORTON: I suggest there is barely one single
word of truth in anything you have said, either to me,
or to the Judge Advocate, or to the Commander. I
suggest that you broke into Elliot's locker, that you
stole the postal order for five shillings belonging to
Elliot, that you cashed it by means of forging his
name—

RONNIE: I didn't. I didn't.

SIR ROBERT MORTON: I suggest that you did it for a joke,
meaning to give Elliot the five shillings back, but that
when you met him and he said he had reported the
matter you got frightened and decided to keep
quiet—

RONNIE: No, no. It isn't true—

SIR ROBERT MORTON: I suggest that by continuing to deny
your guilt you are causing great hardship to your own
family, and considerable annoyance to high and
important persons in this country—

CATHERINE: That's a disgraceful thing to say!

ARTHUR: . . . *sir* . . .

SIR ROBERT MORTON: *(Leaning forward and glaring at*
RONNIE *with the utmost venom)* I suggest, that the
time has at last come for you to undo some of the
misery you have caused by confessing to us all now
that you are a forger, a liar, and a thief!

RONNIE: I'm not! I'm not! I'm not! I didn't do it—

GRACE *has flown to his side and envelops him.*

ARTHUR: This is outrageous, sir—

Beat.

SIR ROBERT *gathers himself together. The phone rings.*
MICHAEL *answers the phone, speaks in a whisper, and*
hangs it up. SIR ROBERT *starts toward the door and walks*
out into MICHAEL's *office. The* CHAUFFEUR *retires, touch-*
ing his cap.

40. INT. MICHAEL'S OFFICE. DAY.
SIR ROBERT MORTON: *(To* DESMOND*)* May I drop you any-
    where, Curry?
DESMOND: Er, no, I . . .
MICHAEL *helps* SIR ROBERT *into a coat.*
SIR ROBERT MORTON: Send all of his files here by tomor-
    row morning.
DESMOND: But, but will you need them now?
SIR ROBERT MORTON: Oh, yes. The boy is plainly innocent.
    I accept the brief.
He bows to ARTHUR *and* GRACE *and* CATHERINE, *and nods*
as he leaves his chambers.

DISSOLVE TO:

41. INT. PRINT SHOP. DAY. (WINTER).
The stove, a fire in the stove. Snow outside the window. The
EDITOR, *in sweater and half mittens, puts up an editorial*
sheet and begins to mark it up. Pan off him to an editorial
cartoon, pasted on the wall; it shows the exterior of a cheap
travelers' hotel and a sign on the outside reading: "No
Children. No Pets. No Discussion of the Winslow Case!"

42. INT. HOUSE OF COMMONS. DAY.
An M.P. *and a* COLLEAGUE *stand near the screen in the pas-*
sageway between the two doors of the House of Com-
mons. MEMBERS *move past them.*

ANGLE. A PACKED HOUSE.

A man, the FIRST LORD, *in his sixties, is on his feet.*

FIRST LORD: The Admiralty, during the whole of this long-drawn-out dispute, has at no time acted hastily or ill-advisedly, and it is a matter of mere histrionic hyperbole for the right honorable and learned gentlemen opposite to characterize the conduct of my department as that of callousness so inhuman as to amount to deliberate malice towards the boy Winslow. Such unfounded accusations I can well choose to ignore.

Interruptions.

ANGLE.

The COLLEAGUE *and the* M.P. *at the screen.*

M.P.: . . . votes to put the question . . .

SIR ROBERT *comes from inside the House, and the two address him. The talk continues by the screen, in the corridor.*

M.P.: *(Cont'd. To Sir Robert)* How important *is* it to you, Bobby?

SIR ROBERT MORTON: How important *is* it . . . Ah, well, it's only important to *win* . . .

COLLEAGUE: . . . shouldn't you be in the House . . . ?

FIRST LORD: *(Off)* I repeat . . .

SIR ROBERT MORTON: . . . long's he's repeating himself, what am I missing out here? Look here: the thing of it is *the Votes.*

We hear the FIRST LORD *continue offscreen.*

FIRST LORD: *(VO)* Honorable Members opposite may interrupt as much as they please, but I repeat—there is nothing whatever that the Admiralty has done, or failed to do, in the case of this cadet for which I, as First Lord, need to apologize.

Further interruptions.

42A. INT. HOUSE OF COMMONS, LOBBY. DAY.

ANGLE.

On CATHERINE, *as she enters the lobby of the House. She hears the* FIRST LORD *and stops, glances at her watch, and begins hurrying.*

ANGLE.

On SIR ROBERT, *the* COLLEAGUE, *and an* M.P.

COLLEAGUE: Well, yes, well. What do you say to that, Tony, do we have the votes?

M.P.: Well, can you *bring* it to a vote, end of the day, it's a fourteen-year-old *boy* . . .

ANGLE.

On CATHERINE *hurrying down the hall. We hear the* FIRST LORD *going on in the BG.*

42B. INT. HOUSE OF COMMONS. DAY.

ANGLE. ON THE FIRST LORD.

FIRST LORD: *(Cont'd.)* The Chief point of criticism against the Admiralty appears to center in the purely legal question of the Petition of Right brought by a Member.

ANGLE.

On SIR ROBERT *et al.* SIR ROBERT *takes a sheet of paper from a* COLLEAGUE, *jots down a note, hands it to a* SERGEANT AT ARMS, *and points into the chamber.*

ANGLE.

On SERGEANT OF ARMS *as he proceeds into the House,*
past the rows of the seated members, toward the FIRST
LORD.

FIRST LORD: *(Cont'd.)* A citizen seeking redress. On behalf
of the Petition of Rights and the demurrer thereto.
This member has made great play of this boy and of
the Admiralty with his address and eloquence.

The note is handed to the FIRST LORD.

FIRST LORD: *(Cont'd.)* And I was moved, as any honorable
member opposite, by his resonant use of the words
"Let Right Be Done" . . .

SIR ROBERT *looks up at the words.*

ANGLE. ON THE FIRST LORD.

FIRST LORD: *(Cont'd.)* "Let Right Be Done" . . .

43. INT. HOUSE OF COMMONS, LOBBY. DAY.

ANGLE.

In the lobby, CATHERINE *hurries up a staircase; a sign next*
to the staircase reads, "Women's Gallery." Various
WOMEN *descending the staircase, one nods to* CATHERINE.

44. INT. HOUSE OF COMMONS, WOMEN'S GALLERY. DAY.

Several WOMEN, *among them the* SUFFRAGETTE *from*
CATHERINE's *office, watching the proceedings.* CATHERINE
sits down behind the screen. The SUFFRAGETTE *turns to*
whisper to her.

SUFFRAGETTE: No, you didn't miss anything.

CATHERINE *nods, takes two apples from her bag, hands*
one to the SUFFRAGETTE, *and they both begin to eat.*

CATHERINE *takes a fruit knife from her pocket and cuts the*

apple. They look through the screen down at the FIRST
LORD. *We hear the* FIRST LORD.

FIRST LORD: *(Cont'd. VO)* The time-honored phrase
   with which in his opinion the Attorney General
   should without question have endorsed Mr.
   Winslow's Petition of Right. Nevertheless, the matter
   is not nearly as simple as he appears to imagine.
   Cadet Ronald Winslow is a servant of the Crown,
   and has therefore no more right than any other member of His . . .

ANGLE. INT. HOUSE OF COMMONS, FLOOR.
On SIR ROBERT. *His eye is caught, he looks up.*

FIRST LORD: *(Cont'd.)* Majesty's forces to sue the Crown
   in open court. To allow him to do so would undoubt-
   edly raise the most dangerous precedents. There is
   no doubt whatever in my mind that in certain cases
   private rights may have to be sacrificed to public
   good.

CATHERINE *picks up her notebook.*

SUFFRAGETTE: He's just been saying all the Great Crimes
   are Committed in the Name of Public Tranquillity.

ANGLE.
On CATHERINE, *as she nods and starts to write in her
book.*

FIRST LORD: *(Cont'd. VO)* . . . this nation, this sea-girt,
   and this sea-*dependent* nation, which relies upon the
   Navy not only for . . .

Several REPORTERS *and* PHOTOGRAPHERS, *lounging on the
street in front of the House, stamping their feet to keep
warm. They huddle around a stove. A* NEWSPAPER BOY
with a placard shouts out, "Winslow case latest."

45. INT. WINSLOW HOUSE, RONNIE'S ROOM. NIGHT.

ANGLE.

On the trunk on which we see RONNIE's *name, but on which "Osbourne" has been painted out.*

ANGLE.

On GRACE *tucking* RONNIE *into his bed.*

RONNIE: *(Asleep)* 'S everything alright, Mother?

GRACE: Everything is fine.

ANGLE.

On ARTHUR, *as he comes into the doorway. He looks on at* GRACE *tucking* RONNIE *into bed. She comes over to him; they speak in whispers.*

ARTHUR: I fancy this might be a good opportunity of talking to Violet.

GRACE: I'll do it one day, Arthur. Tomorrow, perhaps. Not now.

ARTHUR: I believe you'd do better to grasp the nettle. Delay only adds to your worries—

GRACE: *(Bitterly)* My worries? What do you know about my worries?

ARTHUR: A good deal, Grace. But I feel they would be a lot lessened if you faced the situation squarely.

GRACE: *(Pause)* It won't be easy for her to find another place.

ARTHUR: We'll give her an excellent reference.

GRACE: That won't alter the fact.

ARTHUR: *(Sitting on* RONNIE's *trunk)* The facts, at this moment, are that we have half of the income we had a year ago and we're living at nearly the same rate. However you look at it that's bad economics—

GRACE: I'm not talking about economics, Arthur. I'm talking about ordinary, common, or garden facts—things we took for granted a year ago and which now don't seem to matter anymore.

ARTHUR: Such as?

GRACE: Such as a happy home and peace and quiet and an ordinary, respectable life. There's your return for it, I suppose. *(She indicates the headline in the paper.)* I can only pray to God that you know what you're doing.

RONNIE *stirs in his sleep.* GRACE *lowers her voice at the end of her speech.*

   Pause.

ARTHUR: I know exactly what I'm doing, Grace.

GRACE: Do you, Arthur . . . ?

ANGLE.

On ARTHUR, *sitting on* RONNIE's *trunk.*

GRACE: *(Cont'd. VO)* He's perfectly happy, at a good school, doing very well. No one need ever have known about Osbourne, if you hadn't gone and shouted it out to the whole world. As it is, whatever happens now, he'll go through the rest of his life as the boy who stole that postal order—

ANGLE. ON THE TWO OF THEM.

ARTHUR: He didn't steal it, Grace.

GRACE: You talk about sacrificing everything for him; but when he's grown-up he won't thank you for it, Arthur—even though you've given your life to publish his innocence as you call it.

ARTHUR *makes an impatient gesture. He gets up stiffly, and the two move into the upstairs landing.*

46. INT. WINSLOW UPSTAIRS LANDING. NIGHT.

GRACE: *(Cont'd.)* Yes, Arthur—your life. You talk gaily about arthritis and a touch of gout, but you know as well as any of the doctors what's the matter with you. *(Pause)* You're destroying yourself, Arthur, and me and your family besides. For what, I'd like to know? For what, Arthur?

ARTHUR: *(Quietly)* For Justice, Grace.

GRACE: Are you sure it's true? Are you sure it isn't pride and self-importance?

ARTHUR: No, Grace I don't think it is. I really don't think it is—

GRACE: No. This time I'm not going to cry and say I'm sorry, and make it all up again. I can stand anything if there is a reason for it. But for no reason at all, it's unfair to ask so much of me. It's unfair—

ARTHUR *puts an arm around her;* RONNIE *has, meanwhile, opened his eyes.*

RONNIE: What's the matter, Father?

ARTHUR: *(Turning from the door)* Your mother is a little upset.

RONNIE: *(Drowsily)* Why? Aren't things going well?

ARTHUR: Oh, yes. *(Murmuring)* Very well. Very well indeed.

RONNIE *contentedly closes his eyes again.*

ARTHUR: *(Cont'd. Gently)* Go to sleep now, Ronnie.

He sees RONNIE *is asleep again.* ARTHUR *closes* RONNIE's *door.* GRACE *heads to her bedroom.*

47. INT. WINSLOW DINING ROOM/HALLWAY. NIGHT.

ARTHUR *coming downstairs.* VIOLET, *putting a tray of sandwiches on the dining room table.* ARTHUR *enters the dining room.*

ARTHUR: *(Cont'd.)* Thank you, Violet.
There is the sound of the door knocker. VIOLET *turns to*
ARTHUR, *then goes to the door. It is a* POSTMAN; *he hands*
her a letter.

ANGLE. ON VIOLET, TAKING THE LETTER.

ANGLE. ON ARTHUR, WATCHING HER.
She turns and proceeds toward the backstairs.
ARTHUR: *(Cont'd.)* Oh, Violet . . .

ANGLE.
On VIOLET, *holding the letter, at the staircase, about to*
descend to the kitchen; she has picked up her bag of knit-
ting from the newel post. She turns.
VIOLET: Yes, sir.
ARTHUR *walks up to her.*
ARTHUR: How long have you been with us?
VIOLET: Twenty-four years come April, sir.
ARTHUR: As long as that?
VIOLET: Yes, sir. Miss Kate was that high when I first came
    in. *(She indicates a small child.)*—and Mr. Dickie
    hadn't even been thought of—
ARTHUR: *(Pause)* What do you think of this case, Violet?
VIOLET: A fine old rumpus that is, and no mistake.
ARTHUR: It is, isn't it? A fine old rumpus.
VIOLET: There was a bit in the *Evening News.* Did you
    read it, sir?
ARTHUR: No. What did it say?
VIOLET: Oh, about how it was a fuss about nothing and a
    shocking waste of the Government's time, but how it
    was a good thing all the same because it could only
    happen in England—

ARTHUR: There seems to be a certain lack of logic in that argument—

VIOLET: Well, perhaps they put it a bit different, sir. Still, that's what it said all right. And when you think it's all because of our Master Ronnie—I have to laugh about it sometimes. I really do. Wasting the Government's time at his age! I never did. Well, wonders will never cease.

ARTHUR: I know. Wonders will never cease.

VIOLET: Well—would that be all, sir?

ARTHUR: Yes, Violet. That'll be all.

CATHERINE *comes in.*

CATHERINE: Good evening, Violet.

VIOLET: Good evening, miss.

She goes out.

48. INT. WINSLOW HALLWAY/STUDY. NIGHT.

ARTHUR *stands in the hallway with the plate of sandwiches. He puts the letter down.* CATHERINE *moves to and fro from the study, back to her father and the dining room. She takes several sheets of paper from a file. She takes out a ledger, sits at the desk and writes. She takes out her notebook.*

CATHERINE: *(Addressing her father)* Hello, Father.

ARTHUR: And how did it go this evening . . . ?

CATHERINE: . . . I have to transcribe my notes . . .

She writes; she turns on the light at the piano.

ARTHUR: What's happened? Is the debate over?

CATHERINE: As good as. The First Lord gave me an assurance that in the future there would be no inquiry at Osbourne or Dartmouth without informing the parents first. That seemed to satisfy most members—

ARTHUR: But what about *our* case? Is he going to allow us a fair trial?

CATHERINE: Apparently not.

ARTHUR: But that's iniquitous. I thought he would be forced to—

CATHERINE: I thought so, too. The House evidently thought otherwise.

CATHERINE: *(Referring to the plate of sandwiches)* Are those for me?

ARTHUR: Yes.

CATHERINE *passes into the backstairs hallway.*

ARTHUR *joins her and sits down at the window bench.*

49. INT. WINSLOW BACKSTAIRS HALLWAY/HALLWAY. NIGHT.

ARTHUR: *(Cont'd.)* So, we're back where we started.

CATHERINE: I'm sorry, Father?

ARTHUR: I said, We're back where we started, then.

CATHERINE: It looks like it.

She takes VIOLET's *shawl from the banister and puts it on.*

ARTHUR: But didn't Sir Robert make any protest when the First Lord refused a trial?

CATHERINE: Oh, something far more spectacular. He'd had his feet on the Treasury table and his hat over his eyes during most of the First Lord's speech—and he suddenly got up, glared at the First Lord, threw a bundle of notes on the floor, and stalked out of the house. Magnificent effect.

ARTHUR: Or perhaps a display of feeling.

CATHERINE: Sir Robert, Father dear, is not a man of feeling. I don't think any emotion at all can stir that dead heart— And what have we done for *him*? First-rate publicity: The Staunch Defender of the Little Man, and a stick for an ambitious man to beat the Government with. Lucky for him.

ARTHUR: Lucky for us, too.

CATHERINE: Granted, yes, but don't fool yourself. He is an avaricious, a *conniving,* an unfeeling man. We've *bought* his services for the moment . . . we've bought him, like a cheap . . .

VIOLET *enters announcing.*

VIOLET: Sir Robert Morton . . .

Pause.

SIR ROBERT *enters.*

SIR ROBERT MORTON: Good evening.

CATHERINE: *(Choking)* Good evening.

SIR ROBERT MORTON: Something gone down the wrong way?

CATHERINE: Yes.

SIR ROBERT MORTON: May I assist?

He pats her on the back.

CATHERINE: Most kind.

SIR ROBERT MORTON: *(To* ARTHUR*)* Good evening, sir. I thought I would call and give you an account of the day's proceedings, but perhaps your daughter has forestalled me.

ARTHUR: It was very good of you to call, sir. *(To* CATHERINE*)* Will you entertain Sir Robert for a moment . . . ?

CATHERINE: Did you know I was in the gallery?

SIR ROBERT MORTON: With such a charming hat, how could I have missed you?

As ARTHUR *starts to rearrange his attire,* CATHERINE *leads* SIR ROBERT *into the study.*

50. INT. WINSLOW STUDY/HALLWAY. NIGHT.

SIR ROBERT, *standing in the "war room" area, picks up several pamphlets on the Winslow case, pro and con.*

Camera pans them, as INS., and tilts to scan notes tacked to the bookcase.

ANGLE. ON CATHERINE AND SIR ROBERT.

CATHERINE: Will you betray a technical secret, Sir Robert? What happened in the first examination to make you so sure of his innocence?

SIR ROBERT MORTON: Three things. First of all, he made far too many damaging admissions. A guilty person would have been much more careful and on his guard. Secondly, I laid him a trap; and thirdly, left him a loophole. Anyone who was guilty would have fallen into the one and darted through the other. He did neither.

CATHERINE: The trap was to ask him suddenly what time Elliot put the postal order in his locker, wasn't it?

SIR ROBERT MORTON: Yes.

CATHERINE: And the loophole?

SIR ROBERT MORTON: I then suggested to him that he had stolen the postal order for a joke—which, had he been guilty, he would surely have admitted to as being the lesser of two evils.

CATHERINE: I see. It was very cleverly thought out.

SIR ROBERT MORTON: Thank you.

CATHERINE: *(Pause)* And what of the twenty-five minutes?

Pause.

SIR ROBERT MORTON: The twenty-five minutes.

CATHERINE: Ronnie went back to the locker room, and there were twenty-five minutes there which he could not account for. What was he doing?

Pause.

SIR ROBERT MORTON: But I thought *you* should know.

CATHERINE: Why on earth me?

SIR ROBERT MORTON: It is a crime you indulge in. *(He leans closer.)*

ANGLE, TIGHT TWO SHOT AS SIR ROBERT DEMIWHISPERS TO
HER.
SIR ROBERT MORTON: *(Cont'd.)* He was smoking a ciga-
rette.

ANGLE. ON ARTHUR AS HE ENTERS.
CATHERINE *and* SIR ROBERT *move apart.*
ARTHUR: May we offer you some refreshment, Sir Robert?
A whiskey and soda?
SIR ROBERT MORTON: A whiskey, thank you.
CATHERINE *goes out into the hall to look for* VIOLET.
ARTHUR: My daughter has told me of your demonstration
during the First Lord's speech. She described it as—
magnificent.
SIR ROBERT MORTON: Did she? That was good of her. It's a
very old trick, you know. I've done it many times in
the Courts. It's nearly always surprisingly effective—
CATHERINE *catches her father's eye and nods. She starts
for the bellpull at the door.*
SIR ROBERT MORTON: *(Cont'd.)* Was the First Lord at all
put out by it . . . did you notice . . . ?
CATHERINE: How could he have failed to be? I wish you
could have seen it, Father, it was . . .
VIOLET *enters.*
VIOLET: I beg your pardon, sir. I quite walked off and for-
got to give you the letter.
CATHERINE: When did this come, Violet?
VIOLET: A few minutes ago, miss.
She gives the letter to CATHERINE *and exits.*
ARTHUR: Who is it from?
CATHERINE: I shouldn't bother to read it, if I were you.
ARTHUR *looks at her, puzzled, then takes up the letter.*
ARTHUR: *(To* SIR ROBERT*)* Will you forgive me?

SIR ROBERT MORTON: Of course.

ARTHUR *heads for the study to get his glasses.* CATHERINE *follows, leading* SIR ROBERT *with her.* ARTHUR *opens the letter and begins to read.*

51. INT. WINSLOW STUDY/DRAWING ROOM. NIGHT.
CATHERINE *watches her father for a moment, then turns to* SIR ROBERT.

CATHERINE: Well, what do you think the next step should be?

SIR ROBERT MORTON: I believe that the best plan would be to renew our efforts to force the Director of Public Prosecutions to act.

He, too, has his eye on ARTHUR, *sensing something amiss.*

CATHERINE: Father—Sir Robert thinks we might get the Director of Public Prosecutions to act—

ARTHUR: What?

SIR ROBERT MORTON: We were discussing how to proceed with the case—

ARTHUR: The case? *(He stares, a little blankly, from one to the other. To* SIR ROBERT, *abruptly)* I'm afraid I don't think, all things considered, that much purpose would be served by going on—

SIR ROBERT *and* CATHERINE *stare at him blankly.* CATHERINE *goes to him and takes the letter from his lap. She begins to read.*

SIR ROBERT MORTON: But that's absurd. Of course we must go on.

ARTHUR: *(Slowly)* I have made sacrifices for this case. Some of them I had no right to make, but I made them nonetheless. But there is a limit, and I have reached it. I am sorry, Sir Robert. The Winslow Case is now closed.

ARTHUR *exits.*

CATHERINE: Perhaps I should explain this letter.

SIR ROBERT MORTON: There is no need.

CATHERINE: *(To* SIR ROBERT*)* This letter is from a certain Colonel Watherstone, who is the father of the man I'm engaged to. He writes that our efforts to discredit the Admiralty in the House of Commons today have resulted merely in our making the name of Winslow a nationwide laughingstock.

SIR ROBERT MORTON: I don't care for his English.

CATHERINE: It's not very good, is it? He goes on to say that unless my father will give him a firm undertaking to drop this whining and reckless agitation—I suppose he means the case—he will exert every bit of influence he has over his son to prevent him marrying me.

SIR ROBERT MORTON: I see. May I take a cigarette?

CATHERINE: Yes, of course. It's a vile habit—*isn't* it?

SIR ROBERT MORTON: Which of us is perfect. *(Pause)* That really was a most charming hat, Miss Winslow—

CATHERINE: I'm glad you liked it.

SIR ROBERT MORTON: It seems decidedly wrong to me that a lady of your political persuasion should be allowed to adorn herself with such a very feminine allurement. It really looks so awfully like trying to have the best of both worlds—

CATHERINE: Does it, indeed?

SIR ROBERT MORTON: It does.

CATHERINE: And is that a particularly female trait? I'm not a militant, you know, Sir Robert. I don't go about shattering glass or pouring acid down pillar boxes.

SIR ROBERT MORTON: *(Languidly)* I am truly glad to hear it. Both these activities would be highly unsuitable in that hat— *(Pause)* I have never yet fully grasped what active steps you take to propagate your cause, Miss Winslow.

CATHERINE: *(Shortly)* I am an organizing secretary at the West London Branch of the Woman's Suffrage Association.

SIR ROBERT MORTON: Indeed? Is the work hard?

CATHERINE: Very.

SIR ROBERT MORTON: But not, I should imagine, particularly lucrative.

CATHERINE: The work is voluntary and unpaid.

SIR ROBERT MORTON: Dear me! What sacrifices you young ladies seem prepared to make for your convictions. *(He walks* CATHERINE *into the hall. They see* ARTHUR *seated at a stack of papers in the dining room. To* ARTHUR*)* I'm sorry if I spoke to you, sir, with enthusiasm.

ARTHUR: Not at all.

SIR ROBERT MORTON: Might I request that you delay your decision till you've thought on it a while?

ARTHUR: I will give you my answer in a few days.

DISSOLVE TO:

52. EXT. HORSE GUARDS BARRACKS. DAY.
The Guards drilling.

ANGLE.
JOHN WATHERSTONE, *in uniform, approaching an iron fence. Beyond the fence we see* CATHERINE, *holding a large portfolio.*

ANGLE.
On CATHERINE, *as she comes around the fence to meet* JOHN *at a sentry box. The* SENTRY *comes to attention as* JOHN *salutes him, and* CATHERINE *and* JOHN *walk into the Horse Guards' drilling area.*

53. INT. GUARDHOUSE. DAY.

We see drilling through the window.

JOHN: *(Announcing the "theme" of the encounter)* My
     father wrote your father a letter.

CATHERINE: Yes, that's right.

JOHN: You read it?

CATHERINE: Yes. Did you?

JOHN: He showed it to me. *(Pause)* Yes. What's his
     answer?

CATHERINE: My father . . . ?

JOHN: Yes.

CATHERINE: I, I don't suppose he'll send one.

JOHN: He'll ignore it?

CATHERINE: Isn't that the best response to blackmail?

JOHN: Yes . . . it was rather high-handed of the old man . . .

CATHERINE: High-handed?

JOHN: The trouble is—he's serious.

CATHERINE: I never thought he wasn't.

JOHN: If your father keeps on with the case, I'm very much
     afraid he'll do as he threatened.

CATHERINE: Forbid the match?

JOHN: That's right.

CATHERINE: An empty threat, then, isn't it?

JOHN: *(Pause)* Well, there's always the allowance—

CATHERINE: Yes, I see. There's always the allowance.

JOHN: . . . and without your settlement . . . you know I
     can't live on my pay, and, with two of us—

CATHERINE: I've heard it said that two can live as cheaply
     as one.

JOHN: Don't you believe it.

CATHERINE: Yes, I see.

A COLONEL *and a* CAPTAIN *enter the room.*

CAPTAIN: The Bureau forwarded the minutes to the Arms
     Board, and we have a receipted copy of it . . .

COLONEL: Of the note of the fifteenth . . . ?

CAPTAIN: Yes, sir. *(Pause)* Mr. Watherstone.

JOHN: Sir. May I present my fiancée, Miss Winslow.

COLONEL: Ah yes, Miss Winslow . . .

He and CATHERINE *exchange looks.*

JOHN: Permit me to present my fiancée, Miss Winslow.

COLONEL: Miss Winslow.

COLONEL *looks after* JOHN *and* CATHERINE *as they exit.*

EXT. HORSE GUARDS BARRACKS, A PATHWAY. DAY.

JOHN: . . . mannerless fellow . . .

CATHERINE: What do we do now?

ANGLE. EXT. THE ROOM.

JOHN *and* CATHERINE *are walking. Two* SOLDIERS *salute* JOHN.

JOHN: *(Of her briefcase)* Are you off to the House of Commons again?

CATHERINE: Ah, yes. It's hard on you, John. Isn't it . . . ?

Pause.

JOHN *takes out a newspaper and shows it to* CATHERINE.

JOHN: Fellow thought I'd like to see this. Showed it to me.

ANGLE, INS.

The cartoon of John Bull saying, "Can we get some work done around here?"

ANGLE. ON CATHERINE AND JOHN.

CATHERINE: *(Pause)* Do you want to marry me, John?

JOHN: What?

CATHERINE: I said: Do you want to marry me?

JOHN: Have I ever wavered?

CATHERINE: Never before.

JOHN: I'm not wavering now. I'm telling you the course that we should take.

CATHERINE: But isn't it too late? Do you want to marry the Winslow Girl?

JOHN: All that will blow over in time.

CATHERINE: And we'd still have the allowance—

JOHN: *(Quietly)* It is important, darling. I'm sorry, but you can't shame me into saying that it isn't.

CATHERINE: I didn't mean to shame you—

JOHN: Oh, but you *did*.

CATHERINE: *(Pause)* I'm sorry.

JOHN: The case is lost, Catherine. The case is lost. Give it up. *(Pause)* What is your answer?

CATHERINE: I love you, John. The answer is I want to be your wife.

JOHN: *Well*, then. You'll drop the case.

CATHERINE: Yes. I will. I must tell Sir Robert.

54. INT. HOUSE OF COMMONS. DAY.

A MEMBER *reading a newspaper. A subhead reads:*
"Winslow Case, Call for Closure."
   The FIRST LORD *is on his feet.*

FIRST LORD: To continue to squander, to squander, I say, for the time, manpower, public esteem, public *trust*.

While the FIRST LORD *carries on,* SIR ROBERT *gets up, takes his feet across the "White Line," and moves to a bench on which we see several papers. A newspaper headline reads, "Winslow Case: A Call for Closure."*

ANGLE.

On SIR ROBERT, *mopping his brow, sitting in the House.*

FIRST LORD: *(VO)* For a *child*, Gentlemen, for a *child*, a *guilty* child, mind you, to squander *all*, for . . . Sentiment . . . one *can*not sue the Crown, Justice has been done to the tenth decimal point, and it is time to lay aside nursery gossip, and to proceed with the business of Government.

ANGLE. ON THE COLLEAGUE AND SIR ROBERT.
COLLEAGUE: You're all in, Bobby.
SIR ROBERT MORTON: What?
COLLEAGUE: I say you're all in, go home.
M.P.: We're finished, Bob.
COLLEAGUE: You fought the Good Fight. You fought the good fight, but we ain't got the votes. It's over. *(Pause)* Don't break your Heart over it.
M.P.: Everybody loses one. There's no shame in it.
COLLEAGUE: Listen to Tony, Bob.
M.P.: You can't hold back the tide.
SIR ROBERT *nods*.
   In the background we hear the FIRST LORD *go on.*

ANGLE.
On SIR ROBERT, *as he bends to a sheet of paper on the bench, picks it up, and looks at it.*
COLLEAGUE: You couldn't have fought it harder. The House is against you, let it go.

ANGLE, INS.
The sheet music "How, Still, We See Thee Lie, or The Naughty Winslow Boy." We see the picture of RONNIE *holding off the admirals and the lyrics, "How dare you sully Nelson's name for this land did die . . ." et cetera.*

ANGLE.
On SIR ROBERT, *as the* COLLEAGUE *helps him on with his coat.*

FIRST LORD: *(VO)* When I believe I can state, with certainty, that the mood of this House is sure, correct, and supportive of the Admiralty.

The COLLEAGUE *helping* SIR ROBERT *on with his coat holds various papers in his hands. Among them is the sheet music copy of "How, Still, We See Thee Lie." We see* SIR ROBERT *take the sheet music and peruse it.*

ANGLE, INS.

The sheet music, SIR ROBERT's *hand turning it over to read it.*

MEMBER: Put the question.

A MEMBER *comes out of the House and puts a comforting hand on* SIR ROBERT's *shoulder.*

SIR ROBERT MORTON: . . . they're calling the question.

COLLEAGUE: Let them call the question. We're done . . . there's no shame in it, Bob.

ANGLE. IN THE CHAMBER ON THE CHAIRMAN.

CHAIRMAN: The motion is . . .

ANGLE. ON SIR ROBERT IN THE PASSAGEWAY.

SIR ROBERT *puts down the sheet music.*

SIR ROBERT MORTON: Point of order.

ANGLE. ON A MEMBER IN THE HOUSE.

Turning his head to look at SIR ROBERT, *reentering the chamber.*

ANGLE. ON SIR ROBERT.

Reentering the chamber in his coat and hat. Camera takes him to his seat; he is nodding to the CHAIRMAN.

SIR ROBERT MORTON: Point of order, point of order.

FIRST LORD: I'm on my feet!

SIR ROBERT MORTON: Point of order, I say.

FIRST LORD: I'm on my feet.

CHAIRMAN: There is a *motion* that . . .

SIR ROBERT MORTON: Point of *order* . . . I must *insist*.

FIRST LORD: . . . upon what *grounds?*

SIR ROBERT MORTON: Well, sit down and I'll tell you . . .

FIRST LORD: *(Sitting)* . . . make your old speech.

SIR ROBERT MORTON: Thank you. I have a point of order. I should like to read into the record . . . two items. Two items . . . first item: Popular Song of the Day. "How, Still, We See Thee Lie, or The Naughty Winslow Boy." *(He displays the sheet music.)* . . . read it into the record . . . two items. "How dare you sully Nelson's Name Who for this Land Did Die? Oh, Naughty Cadet, for Shame, for Shame. How, still, we see thee lie . . ." *(He lays down the sheet music. To himself)* . . . they suggest our concern for the boy might perhaps tarnish the reputation of Lord Nelson.

Pause.

FIRST LORD: You said two items.

SIR ROBERT MORTON: *(Nods)* The other one is this: It's from a slightly older source. It is this: *"You Shall Not Side with the Great Against the Powerless."*

ANGLE. ON A MEMBER, IN THE STANDS.

MEMBER: Point of order.

ANGLE. ON SIR ROBERT.

SIR ROBERT MORTON: I'm on my feet.

CHAIRMAN: Will you yield?

SIR ROBERT MORTON: I will *not* yield. YOU SHALL NOT SIDE WITH THE GREAT AGAINST THE POWER-LESS. . . . Have you heard those words, Gentlemen?

And do you recognize their source . . . ? And I shall add, from that *same* source, *this* injunction: What you do to the *least* of them, you do to me . . . Now, *Now*, Gentlemen . . . *(He removes his coat.)*

DISSOLVE TO:

55. INT. HOUSE OF COMMONS, LOBBY. DAY.
CATHERINE *coming up the stairs. She enters the lobby, which is buzzing, full of excited* MEN.
REPORTER: *(Overheard in passing as he exits the House.)* Most scathing denunciation of a Government department, ever heard in my life.
CATHERINE: . . . what happened?
REPORTER: What happened . . . ? What happened? The First Lord, thought he was safe. Thought he was safe. Sir Robert spoke, all of a sudden, he's under attack.
CATHERINE: He's under attack, whom?
REPORTER: The First Lord . . . The Admiralty . . . they . . .
MICHAEL, SIR ROBERT's *assistant, has come out of the main chamber and is holding a coat.* CATHERINE *comes over to speak to him through the press of the crowd.*
CATHERINE: What happened?
MICHAEL: It seems, miss, it *seems,* that, rather than risk a division, the First Lord has given an undertaking that he will instruct the Attorney General to endorse the Petition of Right.
He looks over CATHERINE's *shoulders. She turns to see* SIR ROBERT *coming out of the House, congratulated by all.*
MICHAEL: *(Cont'd.)* It means that the case of *Winslow Versus Rex* can, therefore, come to Court.
Pause.
    SIR ROBERT *comes over and puts on his coat.*

SIR ROBERT MORTON: Well, miss. What are my instructions? *(Pause)* Miss Winslow: What are my instructions?

CATHERINE: Do you need my instructions, Sir Robert?
Aren't they already on the petition? Doesn't it say,
"Let Right Be Done"?

Pause.

SIR ROBERT MORTON: Well, then, we must endeavor to see
that it *is.*

DISSOLVE TO:

56. INT. PRINT SHOP. DAY.
Lemonade on the stove. The window open, a PRINTER
wearing a singlet, eating his sandwich, mops his brow.

57. EXT. WINSLOW HOUSE. DAY.
A hot June day, PASSERSBY *in light summer clothes, the
women holding parasols.*

   DICKIE, *aged several years, dressed as a commercial
traveler, carrying a briefcase. Dogging him, a* REPORTER,
scribbling in a notebook.

DICKIE: My views on the case? . . . I can't say that I'm all
that sure I *have* "views" on the case.

REPORTER: You've been following the case in Court?

DICKIE: Been following the case in the papers. Thanks to
you chaps. Just come down from Reading.

REPORTER: Come down for the verdict?

DICKIE: Come down for the verdict— That's right.

*Camera takes them onto the sidewalk opposite the
Winslow House. We see a mass of reporters on the pave-
ment opposite.*

DICKIE: *(Cont'd.)* Good place to've opened a restaurant.
(Pause) Steady clientele, mm?

He starts off across the street.

REPORTER: What's your brother like?

DICKIE: Yes . . . *hot,* eh? *(Wipes his brow.)*

He starts up the stairs, through the REPORTERS.

58. INT. WINSLOW HALLWAY/DINING ROOM. DAY.

DICKIE *enters, goes to a humidor, and takes a cigar.* GRACE
is putting out ARTHUR'*s lunch in the dining room. She
comes out and embraces* DICKIE.

GRACE: You're thinner. I like your new suit.

DICKIE: Off the peg at three and a half guineas. I say—
    does that still go on all the time?

GRACE: Waiting for the verdict.

DICKIE: Where's Kate?

GRACE: Kate takes the morning session, I go in the after-
    noon.

DICKIE: *(Pause)* How's it all going?

GRACE: I don't know. I've been there all four days now and
    I've hardly understood a word.

DICKIE: Will there be room for me?

GRACE: Oh, yes. They reserve places for the family.

DICKIE: How'd Ronnie get on in the witness box?

GRACE: Two days he was cross-examined. Two whole
    days. Imagine it, the poor little pet! I must say he
    didn't seem to mind much. He said two days with the
    Attorney General wasn't nearly as bad as two min-
    utes with Sir Robert. Kate says he made a very good
    impression with the Jury—

DICKIE: How is Kate, Mother?

GRACE: Oh, all right. You heard about John, I suppose—

DICKIE: Yes, that's what I meant. How has she taken it?

GRACE: You can never tell with Kate. She never lets you
    know what she's feeling. We all think he's behaved
    very badly.

She indicates ARTHUR'*s presence on the terrace.* DICKIE
heads out there.

59. EXT. WINSLOW TERRACE/STUDY. DAY.
DICKIE *steps out onto the terrace, and* ARTHUR *walks
slowly toward him.*
ARTHUR: How are you, Dickie?
DICKIE: *(Shaking hands)* Very well, thank you, Father.
DICKIE *proceeds into the study.* ARTHUR *sits by a chair at
the terrace door.*
ARTHUR: Mr. Lamb says you've joined the Territorials.
DICKIE *looks around at various broadsheets and pasted-up
newspapers on the study walls: "The Winslow Case,"
"Response of the Admiralty," a profile of Sir Robert Mor-
ton, et cetera.*
DICKIE: I'm sorry, Father, what?
ARTHUR: Mr. Lamb says you've enlisted, in the Territori-
als.
DICKIE: Yes, Father.
ARTHUR: Why have you done that?
DICKIE: Well, from all accounts there's a fair chance of a
scrap soon. If there is I want to get in on it—
ARTHUR: If there is what you call a scrap you'll do far bet-
ter to stay in the bank—
DICKIE: Oh, no, Father. I mean, the bank's all right—but
still—*(Pause)* How's Catherine?
ARTHUR: Catherine's late. She was in at half past yester-
day.
GRACE *appears at the hallway door. They move toward
her.*

60. INT. WINSLOW STUDY/HALLWAY. DAY.
GRACE: Perhaps they're taking the lunch interval later
today.

ARTHUR: Lunch interval? This isn't a cricket match.
(*Looking at her*) Nor, may I say, is it a matinee at the
Gaiety. Why are you wearing that highly unsuitable
getup?

GRACE: Don't you like it, dear? I think it's Mademoiselle
Dupont's best.

ARTHUR: Grace—your son is facing a charge of theft and
forgery—

GRACE: Oh, dear! It's so difficult! I simply can't be seen in
the same old dress, day after day. (*A thought strikes
her.*) I tell you what, Arthur, I'll wear my black coat
and skirt tomorrow—for the verdict.

ARTHUR: Did you say my lunch was ready?

GRACE: Yes, dear. It's only cold. I did the salad myself. Violet and Cook are at the trial.

DICKIE: Is Violet with you? She was under sentence the
last time I saw you—

GRACE: Neither your father nor I have the courage to tell
her—

ARTHUR: I have the courage to tell her.

GRACE: It's funny that you don't, then, dear.

ARTHUR: You see, Dickie! These taunts of cowardice are
daily flung at my head, but should I take them up I'm
forbidden to move in the matter. Such is the logic of
women.

He goes across the hallway into the dining room. DICKIE
and GRACE *stay in the hallway. They watch* ARTHUR *sit
down and then move away.*

61. INT. WINSLOW HALLWAY. DAY.

DICKIE: Will you take him away after the verdict?

GRACE: He's promised to go into a nursing home.

DICKIE: Will he?

GRACE: How do I know?

DICKIE: But surely, if he loses this time, he's lost for
   good.

GRACE: I can only hope that it's true.

CATHERINE *comes in through the backstairs door.*

CATHERINE: Lord! The heat! Mother, can't you get rid of
   those reporters— Hullo, Dickie.

DICKIE: *(Embracing her)* Hullo, Kate.

CATHERINE: Come to be in at the death?

DICKIE: Is that what it's going to be?

CATHERINE: Looks like it.

ARTHUR: *(Calling from his chair in the dining room)*
   You're late, Catherine.

CATHERINE: I know, Father. I'm sorry. There was such a
   huge crowd. *(Mops her brow. To herself)* I have to
   change . . .

*She starts upstairs, checks her watch, and heads for her
room.*

GRACE: *(Calling after her)* Is there a bigger crowd than yes-
   terday, Kate . . . ?

CATHERINE: *(On the stairs)* Yes, Mother. Far bigger.

GRACE: How did it go this morning?

The camera cranes up with DICKIE *as he climbs the
stairs, looking around and looking back at* ARTHUR *and*
GRACE.

CATHERINE: *(VO)* Sir Robert finished his cross-examination of the postmistress. I thought he'd demolished
   her completely. She admitted she couldn't identify
   Ronnie in the Commander's office. She admitted she
   couldn't be sure of the time he came in. She admitted
   that she was called away to the telephone while he
   was buying his fifteen-and-six postal order, and that
   all Osbourne cadets looked alike to her in their uni-
   forms . . .

62. INT. WINSLOW HOUSE, CATHERINE'S ROOM/UPSTAIRS
LANDING. DAY.

CATHERINE *is doing up her hair.* DICKIE *is standing on the*
landing.

CATHERINE: . . . so that it might quite easily have been
    another cadet who cashed the five shillings. It was a
    brilliant cross-examination. He didn't bully her, or
    frighten her—he just coaxed her into tying herself
    into knots. Then, when he'd finished the Attorney
    General asked her again whether she was absolutely
    positive that the same boy that bought the fifteen-
    and-six postal order also cashed the five-shilling one.
    She said yes. She was quite, quite sure because Ronnie
    was such a good-looking little boy that she had spe-
    cially noticed him. She hadn't said that in her exami-
    nation in chief. I could see those twelve good men and
    true nodding away to each other. I believe it undid the
    whole of that magnificent cross-examination.

GRACE *has come into the doorway.*

GRACE: If she thought him so especially good-looking,
    why couldn't she identify him the same evening?

GRACE *hands* CATHERINE *a cup of tea.*

CATHERINE: Don't ask me. Ask the Attorney General. I'm
    sure he has a beautifully reasonable answer.

DICKIE: Ronnie good-looking! What utter rot! She must
    be lying, that woman.

GRACE: Nonsense, Dickie! I thought he looked very well in
    the box yesterday, didn't you, Kate?

CATHERINE: Yes, Mother.

DICKIE: Who else gave evidence for the other side?

DICKIE *walks downstairs.*

CATHERINE: The Commander, the Chief Petty Officer, and
    one of the boys at the college.

DICKIE: Anything very damaging?

CATHERINE: Nothing that we didn't expect.

CATHERINE *emerges from her room with her cup of tea. Her hair is up.*

GRACE: Did you see anybody interesting in Court, dear?

CATHERINE: Yes, Mother. John Watherstone.

GRACE: John? I hope you didn't speak to him, Kate.

CATHERINE: Of course I did.

GRACE: Kate, how could you! What did he say?

CATHERINE: He wished us luck.

GRACE: What impertinence!

ARTHUR: *(Offscreen)* Grace—you will be late for the resumption.

GRACE: *(To herself)* I wonder if Violet will remember to pick up those onions. Perhaps I'd better do it on the way back from the Court.

GRACE: *(Pause)* Kate, dear, I'm so sorry—

CATHERINE: What for, Mother?

GRACE: John proving such a bad hat. I never did like him very much, you know.

CATHERINE: No, I know.

They head downstairs.

63. INT. WINSLOW HALLWAY. DAY.

ARTHUR *examines* DICKIE.

ARTHUR: You look very well. A trifle thinner, perhaps—

DICKIE: Hard work, Father.

ARTHUR: Or late hours?

DICKIE: You can't keep late hours in Reading.

ARTHUR: You could keep late hours anywhere. I've had quite a good report about you from Mr. Lamb.

DICKIE: I took him racing last Saturday. Had the time of his life and lost his shirt.

ARTHUR: Did he?

GRACE *and* CATHERINE *appear.*

GRACE: Now, Dickie, when you get to the front door put your head down, like me, and just charge through them all.

ARTHUR: Why don't you go out by the garden?

GRACE: I wouldn't like to risk this dress getting through the roses. Come on, Dickie. I always shout: "I'm the maid and don't know nothing," so don't be surprised.

DICKIE: Righto, Mother.

GRACE *goes out.* DICKIE *follows her.* CATHERINE'*s hair falls. She sighs and starts to put it up again. She heads into the dining room toward the terrace.* ARTHUR *follows.*

64. INT./EXT. WINSLOW DRAWING ROOM/TERRACE. DAY.

ARTHUR: Are we going to lose the case, Kate?

CATHERINE *does not reply. She sips her cup of tea and lights a cigarette.*

ARTHUR: *(Cont'd.)* How is Sir Robert? The papers said that he began today by telling the judge he felt ill and might have to ask for an adjournment. I trust he won't collapse—

CATHERINE: He won't. It was just another of those brilliant tricks of his that he's always boasting about. It got him the sympathy of the Court and possibly—no, I won't say that—

ARTHUR: Say it.

CATHERINE: *(Slowly)* Possibly provided him with an excuse if he's beaten.

ARTHUR: . . . I see.

CATHERINE *looks out at the garden.*

ANGLE, CATHERINE'S POV.

DESMOND *appears at the garden gate.* CATHERINE *and* ARTHUR *turn and see him.*

DESMOND: I trust you do not object to me employing this
    rather furtive entry. The crowds at the front door are
    most alarming—
ARTHUR: Come in, Desmond. Why have you left the
    Court?
DESMOND: My partner will be holding the fort. He is per-
    fectly competent, I promise you.
ARTHUR: I'm glad to hear it.
DESMOND: I wonder if I might see Catherine alone. I have
    a matter of some urgency to communicate to her—
ARTHUR: Oh. Do you wish to hear this urgent matter,
    Kate?
CATHERINE: Yes, Father.
ARTHUR: Very well. I shall finish my lunch.

ARTHUR *retires.*

65. EXT. WINSLOW GARDEN. DAY.
Pause.
DESMOND: *(Checks his watch)* I have to be back in Court.
    Perhaps you would stroll with me. Out in the garden.
DESMOND *and* CATHERINE *walk and then sit down.*
CATHERINE: Yes, Desmond?
DESMOND: It occurred to me during the lunch recess that I
    had far better see you today.
CATHERINE: *(Her thoughts far distant)* Why?
DESMOND: I have a question to put to you, Kate, which, if
    I had postponed putting until after the verdict, you
    might—who knows—have thought had been
    prompted by pity—if we had lost. Or—if we had
    won, your reply might—again who knows—have
    been influenced by gratitude. Do you follow me, Kate?
CATHERINE: Yes, Desmond. I think I do.
DESMOND: Ah. Then possibly you have some inkling of
    what the question is I have to put to you?

CATHERINE: Yes. I think I have.

DESMOND: Oh.

CATHERINE: I'm sorry, Desmond. I ought, I know, to have followed the usual practice in such cases, and told you I had no inkling whatever.

DESMOND: No, no. Your directness and honesty are two of the qualities I so much admire in you. I am glad you have guessed. It makes my task the easier— The *facts* are these: that you don't love me, and never can. And that I love you, and I always will. *(Pause)* It is a situation which, after most careful consideration, I am fully prepared to accept. I reached this decision some months ago, but thought at first it would be better to wait until this case, which is so much on all our minds, should be over. Then at lunch today I determined to anticipate the verdict tomorrow.

Pause.

CATHERINE: *(At length)* I see. Thank you, Desmond. That makes everything much clearer.

DESMOND: There is much more that I had meant to say, but I shall put it in a letter.

CATHERINE: Yes, Desmond. Do. Will you give me a few days to think it over?

DESMOND: Of course. Of course.

CATHERINE: I need hardly tell you how grateful I am, Desmond.

DESMOND: *(A trifle bewildered)* There is no need, Kate. No need at all—

They walk out of the garden.

66. EXT. ALLEYWAY TO STREET. DAY.

CATHERINE *and* DESMOND *enter an alleyway, at the end of which is a taxi.*

CATHERINE: You mustn't keep your taxi waiting—

DESMOND: Then I may expect your answer in a few days?

CATHERINE: Yes, Desmond.

DESMOND: *(Looking at his watch)* I must get back to Court. *(Pause)* How did you think it went this morning?

CATHERINE: I thought the postmistress restored the Admiralty's case with that point about Ronnie's looks—

DESMOND: Oh, no, no. Not at all. There is still the overwhelming fact that she couldn't identify him. What a brilliant cross-examination, was it not?

CATHERINE: Brilliant.

DESMOND: A strange man, Sir Robert. At times, so cold and distant and—and—

CATHERINE: Passionless.

DESMOND: And yet he has a real passion about this case.

CATHERINE: Does he?

DESMOND: I happen to know—of course this must on no account go any further—but I happen to know that he has made a very, very great personal sacrifice in order to bring it to Court.

CATHERINE: Sacrifice? What? Of another brief?

DESMOND: No, no. That is no sacrifice to him. No—he was offered—you really promise to keep this to yourself?

CATHERINE: My dear Desmond, whatever the Government offered him can't be as startling as all that; he's in the opposition.

DESMOND: Indeed. Therefore, a most, most gracious compliment.

CATHERINE: . . . and what position was he offered . . . ?

DESMOND *looks around, leans forward, and whispers to* CATHERINE.

Pause.

  CATHERINE's *eyes widen.*

DESMOND: Yes. That's right. And he turned it down. Simply in order to carry on with the case *Winslow Versus Rex*. Strange are the ways of men, are they not? Good-bye, my dear.

DESMOND *gets in the taxi and drives off. Hold on* CATHERINE.

67. INT. WINSLOW STUDY. DAY.

ARTHUR *is perched on the table reading his Bible.*
    CATHERINE *enters and wanders through to the hallway.*

CATHERINE: Father, I've been a fool.

ARTHUR: Have you, my dear?

CATHERINE: An utter fool.

ARTHUR: In default of further information, I can only repeat, have you, my dear?

CATHERINE: There can be no further information. I'm under a pledge of secrecy.

ARTHUR: What did Desmond want?

CATHERINE: To marry me.

ARTHUR: I trust the folly you were referring to wasn't your acceptance of him?

CATHERINE: Would it be such folly, though?

ARTHUR: Lunacy.

CATHERINE: I'm nearly thirty, you know.

ARTHUR: Thirty isn't the end of life.

CATHERINE: . . . is that so . . . ?

ARTHUR: Better far to live and die an old maid than to marry Desmond.

CATHERINE: Even an old maid must eat.

Pause.

ARTHUR: Did you take my suggestion as regards your Suffrage Association?

CATHERINE: Yes, Father.

ARTHUR: You demanded a salary?

CATHERINE: I asked for one.

ARTHUR: And they're going to give it to you, I trust?

CATHERINE: Two pounds a week. *(Pause)* No, Father. The choice is quite simple. Either I marry Desmond and settle down into quite a comfortable and not really useless existence—or I go on for the rest of my life earning two pounds a week in the service of a hopeless cause.

ARTHUR: A hopeless cause? I've never heard you say that before.

CATHERINE: I've never felt it before. *(Pause)* John's going to get married next month.

She moves to the hallway and sits. ARTHUR *follows.*

68. INT. WINSLOW HALLWAY. DAY.

CATHERINE *is sitting on the stairs.* ARTHUR *stands next to her.*

ARTHUR: Did he tell you?

CATHERINE: Yes. He was very apologetic.

ARTHUR: Apologetic!

CATHERINE: He didn't need to be. It's a girl I know slightly. She'll make him a good wife.

ARTHUR: Is he in love with her?

CATHERINE: No more than he was with me. Perhaps, even, a little less.

ARTHUR: Why is he marrying her so soon after—after—

CATHERINE: After jilting me? Because he thinks there's going to be a war. If there is, his regiment will be among the first to go overseas. She's a general's daughter. Very, very suitable.

ARTHUR: Poor Kate. I'm so sorry, Kate. I'm so sorry.

CATHERINE: We both knew what we were doing. *(She looks at her watch and gets up to go outside.)* If you could go back, Father, and choose again—would your choice be different?

ARTHUR: Perhaps.

CATHERINE: I don't think so.

ARTHUR: I don't think so, either.

CATHERINE: I still say we both knew what we were doing. And we were right to do it.

ARTHUR *kisses the top of her head.*

ARTHUR: Dear Kate. Thank you.

There is silence. A NEWSBOY *can be heard dimly, shouting from the street outside.*

ARTHUR: *(Cont'd.)* You aren't going to marry Desmond, are you?

CATHERINE: In the words of the Prime Minister, Father— wait and see.

He squeezes her hand. The NEWSBOY *can still be heard— now a little louder.*

ARTHUR: What's that boy shouting, Kate?

CATHERINE: Only—"Winslow Case—Latest."

ARTHUR: It didn't sound to me like "Latest."

69. ANGLE. EXT. WINSLOW HOUSE. DAY.
On the street, a BOY *hawking papers, shouting, "Winslow Case Result."*

ANGLE. INS. THE BANNER HEADLINE "WINSLOW CASE RESULT."

70. INT. WINSLOW HALLWAY/DRAWING ROOM/STUDY. DAY.

ARTHUR: Result?

CATHERINE: . . . there must be some mistake.

There is a noise in the hall, and they turn to look as VIOLET *comes in the back door with a bundle of newspapers.*

VIOLET: Oh, sir, oh sir . . .

ARTHUR: What's happened?

VIOLET *heads into the drawing room and puts down the newspapers.* ARTHUR *follows.* CATHERINE *remains in the hallway.*

VIOLET: Oh, Miss Kate. Oh, Miss Kate. Just after they come back from lunch, and Mrs. Winslow she wasn't there neither, nor Master Ronnie. The shouting and the carrying-on—you never heard anything like it in all your life—and Sir Robert standing there at the table with his wig on crooked and the tears running down his face—running down his face they were. Cook and me we did a bit of crying too. Everyone was cheering and the judge kept shouting, but it wasn't any good, because even the Jury joined in, and some of them climbed out of the box to shake hands with Sir Robert. And then outside in the street it was just the same—you couldn't move for the crowd, and you'd think they'd all gone mad the way they were carrying on. Some of them were shouting, "Good old Winslow!" And singing, "For He's a Jolly Good Fellow," and Cook had her hat knocked off again. Oh, it was lovely! *(To* ARTHUR*)* Well, sir, you must be feeling nice and pleased, now it's all over?

ARTHUR: Yes, Violet. I am.

VIOLET: That's right. I always said it would come all right in the end, didn't I?

ARTHUR: Yes. You did.

VIOLET: Two years it's been, now, since Master Ronnie come back that day. Fancy.

ARTHUR: Yes.

VIOLET: I don't mind telling you, sir, I wondered sometimes whether you and Miss Kate weren't just wasting your time carrying on the way you have all the time. Still—you couldn't have felt that if you'd been in Court today— *(She turns to go and stops.)* Oh, sir, Mrs. Winslow asked me to remember most particular to pick up some onions from the greengrocer, but—

CATHERINE: That's all right, Violet. I think Mrs. Winslow is picking them up herself, on her way back—

VIOLET: I see, miss. Poor Madam! What a sell for her when she gets to the Court and finds it's all over. Well, sir—congratulations, I'm sure.

ARTHUR: Thank you, Violet.

VIOLET *leaves the room, and* CATHERINE *enters.*

ARTHUR: *(Cont'd.)* It would appear, then, that we've won.

CATHERINE: Yes, Father, it would appear that we've won.

ARTHUR: *(Slowly)* I would have liked to have been there.

Enter VIOLET.

VIOLET: *(Announcing)* Sir Robert Morton!

SIR ROBERT *walks into the room, mopping his brow. Exit* VIOLET.

SIR ROBERT MORTON: I thought you might like to hear the actual terms of the Attorney General's statement— *(He pulls out a scrap of paper from his cigarette case and moves toward the study.)* So I jotted it down for you. *(Reading)* "I say now, on behalf of the Admiralty, that I accept the declaration of Ronald Arthur Winslow that he did not write the name on the postal order, that he did not take it, and that he did not cash it, and that consequently he was innocent of the charge which was brought against him two years ago. I make that statement without any reservation of any description, intending it to be a complete acceptance of the boy's statements."

He folds the paper up and hands it to ARTHUR.

ARTHUR: Thank you, sir. It is rather hard for me to find the words I should speak to you.

SIR ROBERT MORTON: Pray do not trouble yourself to search for them, sir. Let us take these rather tiresome and conventional expressions of gratitude for granted, shall we? Now, on the question of damages and costs. I fear we shall find the Admiralty rather niggardly. You are likely still to be left considerably out of pocket. However, doubtless we can apply a slight spur to the First Lord's posterior in the House of Commons—

ANGLE, INS.

ARTHUR *removes the offending letter from beneath the magnifying glass. He moves into his study and stands by the terrace door.* CATHERINE *moves to join* SIR ROBERT.

ARTHUR: Please, sir—no more trouble—I beg. Let the matter rest here. *(He shows the piece of paper.)* This is all I have ever asked for.

SIR ROBERT MORTON: *(Turning to* CATHERINE*)* A pity you were not in Court, Miss Winslow. The verdict appeared to cause quite a stir.

CATHERINE: So I heard. Why did the Admiralty throw up the case?

SIR ROBERT MORTON: It was a foregone conclusion. Once the handwriting expert had been discredited—not for the first time in legal history—I knew we had a sporting chance, and no jury in the world would have convicted on the postmistress's evidence.

CATHERINE: But this morning you seemed so depressed.

SIR ROBERT MORTON: Did I? The heat in the courtroom was very trying, you know. Perhaps I was a little fatigued.

SIR ROBERT *mops his brow and sits down. Enter* VIOLET.

VIOLET: *(To* ARTHUR*)* Oh, sir, the gentlemen at the front door say please will you make a statement. They say they won't go away until you do.

ARTHUR: Very well, Violet. Thank you.

VIOLET: Yes, sir.

Exit VIOLET.

ARTHUR: What shall I say?

SIR ROBERT MORTON: *(Indifferently)* I hardly think it matters. Whatever you say will have little bearing on what they write.

ARTHUR: What shall I say, Kate?

CATHERINE: You'll think of something, Father.

ARTHUR: *(To* CATHERINE*)* May I have my stick, please?

CATHERINE: Yes, Father.

CATHERINE *gets his stick for him.*

ARTHUR: How is this? I am happy to have lived long enough to have seen Justice done to my son—

CATHERINE: It's a little gloomy, Father. You're going to live for ages yet—

ARTHUR: Am I? Wait and see. I could say: This victory is not mine; it is the people who have triumphed—as they will always triumph—over despotism. How does that strike you, sir? A trifle pretentious, perhaps.

SIR ROBERT MORTON: Perhaps, sir. I should say it, nonetheless. It will be very popular.

ARTHUR: Perhaps I shall just say what I feel, which is, Thank God We Beat 'Em . . . *(He starts toward the door.)*

71. INT. WINSLOW STUDY. DAY.

SIR ROBERT MORTON: Miss Winslow—might I be rude enough to ask you for a little more of your excellent whiskey?

CATHERINE: Of course.

She goes to get the whiskey. SIR ROBERT, *left alone, sub-sides into a chair. When* CATHERINE *comes back with his whiskey, he does not rise.*

SIR ROBERT MORTON: That is very kind. Perhaps you would forgive me not getting up? The heat in that courtroom was really so infernal.

He takes the glass from her and drains it quickly. She notices his hand trembling slightly.

CATHERINE: Are you feeling all right, Sir Robert?

SIR ROBERT MORTON: Just a slight nervous reaction— that's all. Besides, I have not been feeling myself all day. I told the Judge so, this morning, if you remember, but I doubt if he believed me. He thought it was a trick. What suspicious minds people have, have they not?

CATHERINE: Yes.

SIR ROBERT MORTON: *(Handing her back the glass)* Thank you.

CATHERINE *puts the glass down, then turns to face him.*

CATHERINE: Sir Robert—I'm afraid I have a confession and an apology to make to you.

SIR ROBERT MORTON: Dear lady, I'm sure the one is rash and the other is superfluous. I would far rather hear neither—

CATHERINE: I am afraid you must. This is probably the last time I shall see you, and it is a better penance for me to say this than to write it. I have entirely misjudged your attitude to this case, and if in doing so I have ever seemed to you either rude or ungrateful, I am sincerely and humbly sorry.

SIR ROBERT MORTON: *(Indifferently)* My dear Miss Winslow, you have never seemed to me either rude or ungrateful. And my attitude to this case has been the same as yours—a determination to win at all costs.

Only—when you talk of gratitude—you must remember that those costs were not mine, but yours.

CATHERINE: Weren't they also yours, Sir Robert?

SIR ROBERT MORTON: I beg your pardon?

CATHERINE: Haven't you too made a certain sacrifice for the case?

Pause.

SIR ROBERT MORTON: The robes of that office would not have suited me.

CATHERINE: Wouldn't they?

SIR ROBERT MORTON: And what is more, I fully intend to have Curry censured for revealing a confidence. I must ask you never to divulge it to another living soul, and even to forget it yourself.

CATHERINE: I shall never divulge it. I'm afraid I can't promise to forget it myself.

SIR ROBERT MORTON: Very well. If you choose to endow an unimportant incident with a romantic significance, you are perfectly at liberty to do so.

Sounds of cheering from outside.

SIR ROBERT MORTON: *(Cont'd.)* Could you show me out a back way?

He gets up and goes toward the hallway. CATHERINE *follows.*

72. INT. WINSLOW HALLWAY. DAY.

SIR ROBERT *picks up his hat when* RONNIE *comes in. He is fifteen now, and there are distinct signs of an incipient man-about-town. He is very smartly dressed in a lounge suit and homburg hat.*

RONNIE: I say, Sir Robert, I'm most awfully sorry. I didn't know anything was going to happen.

SIR ROBERT MORTON: Where were you?

RONNIE: At the pictures.

SIR ROBERT MORTON: Pictures.

CATHERINE: Cinematograph.

RONNIE: I'm most awfully sorry. I say, we won. Didn't we?

SIR ROBERT MORTON: Yes. We won.

RONNIE: *(To himself)* How about that. . . . We won . . .
    (He starts out the door.)

73. ANGLE. EXT. WINSLOW HOUSE. DAY.
ARTHUR *stands in front of a cheering crowd. He stills the cheering.*

ARTHUR: This victory . . . these events . . . These
    events . . .

The cheering intensifies. ARTHUR *turns to see* RONNIE *coming through the door, and he puts his arm around him.*

74. ANGLE. EXT. GARDEN. DAY.
SIR ROBERT *and* CATHERINE *can hear the cheering.* SIR
ROBERT *shrugs and takes out a cigarette.*

CATHERINE: Why are you always at such pains to prevent
    people knowing the truth about you, Sir Robert?

SIR ROBERT MORTON: Am I, indeed?

CATHERINE: You know you are. Why?

SIR ROBERT MORTON: Which of us knows the truth about
    himself?

CATHERINE: That is no answer.

SIR ROBERT MORTON: My dear Miss Winslow, are you
    cross-examining me?

CATHERINE: On this point. Why are you ashamed of your
    emotions?

SIR ROBERT MORTON: To fight a case on emotional
    grounds, Miss Winslow, is the surest way to lose it.
    Emotions cloud the issue. Cold, clear logic wins the
    day.

CATHERINE: Was it cold, clear logic that made you weep today at the verdict?

They stop at the garden gate.

SIR ROBERT MORTON: I wept today because right had been done.

CATHERINE: Not Justice?

SIR ROBERT MORTON: No. Not Justice. Right. Easy to do Justice—very hard to do right. Now, I must leave the witness box. I hope I shall see you again. One day, perhaps, in the House of Commons, up in the Gallery.

CATHERINE: Yes, Sir Robert. In the House of Commons, one day, but not up in the Gallery. Across the Floor. One day.

SIR ROBERT MORTON: You still pursue your Feminist activities?

CATHERINE: Oh, yes.

SIR ROBERT MORTON: A pity. It's a lost cause.

CATHERINE: Do you really think so, Sir Robert? How little you know women. *(Pause)* Good-bye. I doubt that we shall meet again.

SIR ROBERT MORTON: Oh. Do you really think so, Miss Winslow? *(Pause)* How little you know men.

FADE OUT.